TURNING THE PAGES OF TEXAS

Other Books by Lonn Taylor

Marfa for the Perplexed

Texas, My Texas: Musings of the Rambling Boy

Texas People, Texas Places: More Musings of the Rambling Boy

The Star-Spangled Banner: The Making of an American Icon

Indian Lodge, Davis Mountains State Park: History and Architecture

The Star-Spangled Banner: The Flag that Inspired the National Anthem

Texas Furniture: The Cabinet Makers and their Work, 1840-1880
(with David B. Warren)

The American Cowboy

New Mexican Furniture
(with Dessa Bokides)

TURNING THE PAGES OF TEXAS

LONN TAYLOR

with a foreword by
Steven L.Davis

Fort Worth, Texas

Library of Congress Cataloging-in-Publication Data

Names: Taylor, Lonn, 1940- author. | Davis, Steven L., writer of foreword.
Title: Turning the pages of Texas / Lonn Taylor ; foreword by Steven L. Davis.
Description: Fort Worth, Texas : TCU Press, [2019] |
Identifiers: LCCN 2018051249 (print) | LCCN 2018053360 (ebook) | ISBN 9780875657202 () | ISBN 9780875657165 | ISBN 9780875657165?q(alk. paper)
Subjects: LCSH: Books--Texas--History. | Book collecting--Texas. | Book collectors--Texas. | Authors--Texas--Biography. | Texas--History. | LCGFT: Book reviews. | Essays.
Classification: LCC Z1003.3.T4 (ebook) | LCC Z1003.3.T4 T39 2019 (print) | DDC 002.09764--dc23
LC record available at https://urldefense.proofpoint.com/v2/url?u=https-3A__lccn.loc.gov_2018051249&d=DwIFAg&c=7Q-FWLBTAxn3T_E3HWrzGYJrC4RvUoWDrzTlitGRH_A&r=O2eiy819IcwTGuw-vrBGiVdmhQxMh2yxeggw9qlTUDE&m=ylppZxaoJBjT4awV_RWIzj5kAiB2GWQTDVKstZDZu5s&s=qyXVSra2gicUHIAiPM3q4OYCcRHu-Io-1GVDw2UG7So&e=

TCU Press
TCU Box 298300
Fort Worth, Texas 76129
817.257.7822
http://www.prs.tcu.edu
To order books:1.800.826.8911

designed & illustrated by
Barbara Mathews Whitehead

✣

For Sherry Kafka Wagner

CONTENTS

III. BACK ROADS AND DARK CORNERS

IV. COOKS, PHOTOGRAPHERS, POETS, AND OTHERS

FOREWORD

AT THE EDGE of Fort Davis, just beneath the volcanic palisades of Sleeping Lion Mountain, sits a modest, enchilada-colored house. To the casual observer, the structure appears unremarkable, box-shaped, and surrounded by prickly pear and ocotillo. Yet to step inside is to enter a wonderland: a beautiful residence overflowing with art and bulging with books, filled with natural light and warmed by the laughter of Lonn Taylor and his gracious wife, Dedie.

The Taylors' welcoming home is a magnet for artists, writers, musicians, historians—anyone who can tell a good story or contribute to a lively conversation. At an elevation of 5,000 feet, this is some of the loftiest talk in Texas. Many evenings, the Taylors can be found hosting a gathering of ample minds in their living room or on their shaded patio. Lonn, as always, presides over the discussions. He excels at drawing out the best in others, and his marvelous, deep-chested laugh—which sounds like a barred owl crossed with bull sea lion—can be heard echoing off the nearby mountains.

The real pleasure of these gatherings is hearing Lonn talk. He is a master storyteller with a deep well of material, for he has been friends with everyone from Janis Joplin to Miss Ima Hogg. He also possesses an expansive and illuminating knowledge on a dazzling array of topics, distilled from a lifetime of voracious reading.

I'm not going to claim that the social affairs at the Taylors are the equivalent of Gertrude Stein's famous salon in Paris in the 1920s, where Ernest Hemingway and F. Scott Fitzgerald traded ripostes with Pablo Picasso and James Joyce—but for West Texas it's pretty dang close. And there's one key difference. As Lonn points out, "I suspect we have more fun than Gertrude Stein did."

For years, Lonn has been charming readers with his "Rambling Boy" musings, his popular weekly column in the *Big Bend Sentinel* that is also broadcast on Marfa Public Radio. He's gathered a wide following of admirers, becoming Texas's Patron Saint for the Intellectually Curious. Anyone who reads Lonn's words or listens to him speak comes away feeling both entertained and enlightened. Who else could describe a book on the subject of cattle brands by making the following observation: "Texans have always been a little nutty about cattle brands, regarding them not as mere marks of ownership on cattle but as prairie equivalents of the coat-of-arms displayed by English aristocrats."

Lonn's columns have always been informed by his eclectic reading, and he maintains an abiding affection for Texas books and authors. He is, in fact, one of our leading experts on Texas literature. He is as well versed in the classics as he is aware of rare and little-known jewels that deserve our attention. In *Turning the Pages of Texas*, Lonn shares the best of his writing about Texas books and authors. He tells us of volumes that range from ancient Pecos River rock art to modern ranch photography, from quilt makers to punk rockers, from a captivating diary kept by a Mexican American soldier during World War I to the tragic story of a Texas writer who died in an insane asylum after publishing her only book in France.

Lonn's writings are guided by more than his authoritative understanding of Texas. He is also a generous spirit, and he has made it a point to get to know many Texas writers personally. His accounts are chock-full of insider information and behind-the-scenes nuggets, gleaned from interviews with authors. He winds everything together in his warm, conversational voice. As a reader, you feel as though you are a guest inside the Taylors' Fort Davis home, and you have adjourned to the patio after dinner, where Lonn has taken a seat in the chair next to yours, his eyes brightening in delight as he uncorks a fresh story.

Before retiring to Fort Davis with Dedie a dozen-plus years ago, Lonn enjoyed a very successful career as a nationally respected historian and museum curator, mounting highly praised exhibitions at the Smithsonian in Washington, DC. Yet paradoxically, this folksy, erudite Texan is now gaining far more public attention as a "retiree" than he ever did at the Smithsonian. He's appeared on Stephen Colbert's TV program, *The Colbert Report,* trading wits with the irreverent host and charming him as easily as he charms readers and visitors to his home. He is featured in newspaper stories and magazine articles across the nation. His *Rambling Boy* podcast is winning him listeners around the globe. Lonn's persona, so deeply authentic and quintessentially Texan, is becoming more famous by the day. In fact, by this point it's probably safe to say that Lonn Taylor has become the Big Bend's best-known personality since the postmodern minimalist artist Donald Judd.

Only something tells me that Lonn has a lot more fun than Donald Judd ever did.

You will have fun, too, reading this book.

Steven L. Davis
San Marcos, Texas
May 2018

Steven L. Davis is a PEN USA award-winning author, past president of the Texas Institute of Letters, and longtime literary curator at the Wittliff Collections, Texas State University.

INTRODUCTION

I ACQUIRED MY first Texas book when I was three years old. It was Siddie Joe Johnson's children's history of Texas, *Texas, Land of the Tejas*, with illustrations by Fanita Lanier. It was a gift from my parents at Christmas of 1943, a reminder that we were Texans even though we were living in South Carolina, where my father was stationed during the war. I learned to read from it, and I learned about the Lady in Blue, and Jean Lafitte, and San Jacinto, and Spindletop, and the Texans in the Flying Tigers from Lanier's unforgettable color illustrations, which were scattered across the pages like bright flower petals.

By the time I was seven I had also acquired copies of J. Frank Dobie's *Legends of Texas*, as related in these pages, as well as my cousin Amelia Williams's *Following Sam Houston*, signed by her, and an odd book called *Sixty Years in the Nueces Valley* by a Mrs. S. G. Miller, who was a girlhood friend of my grandmother Taylor. What is odd about it is that it was published by the Naylor Company in San Antonio, a vanity press, in 1930, and it is bound with another book, *Autobiography of a Revolutionary Soldier*, by John M. Roberts, which has nothing to do with Texas but is the memoir of a South Carolinian who fought in the American Revolution. Perhaps the possession of this volume at such an early age is responsible for my proclivity for oddities in Texana.

These four volumes constituted my Texana bookshelf until we moved to Fort Worth when I was sixteen, and I set out to learn something about my Texas heritage. I discovered Barber's Bookstore and the Fort Worth-Tarrant County Collection of the Fort Worth Public Library at approximately the same time, and they were conveniently close to each other, so that I could sample

Texas books on the library shelves and then try to find copies of any I wanted to own at Barber's. I suppose I could say that Barber's owner, Bryan Perkins, was my first mentor in collecting Texana, although he never advised me not to buy something.

I continued to accumulate Texana through my college years, but my knowledge of the subject took a great leap forward when, in my late twenties, I took a job as an editor and research associate with the Texas State Historical Association. One of my tasks was to check every footnote in every article accepted for the *Southwestern Historical Quarterly*, which the association published. At that time the association was housed on the campus of the University of Texas at Austin on the first floor of the Barker Texas History Library (now Battle Hall), and so every morning I would go upstairs to the largest library of Texana in the world and spend the day padding around its marble floor in my stocking feet pulling books off its shelves. After two years I was familiar with all of the major published works of Texas history and most of the minor ones.

Another part of my job was to catalogue the donations that were received for the association's annual Texana book auction and to send out the thank-you letters for those donations, and through that task I got to know some of Texas's major Texana dealers and collectors, including Morris Cook, Ray Walton, Dorothy Sloan, Johnny Jenkins, Ben Pingenot, Al Lowman, Jenkins Garrett, and J. P. Bryan, Jr.

It was while I was with the association that I developed an interest in a specialized branch of Texana: privately printed pamphlets. One Saturday afternoon I was having a cold beer at the inside bar of the Scholz Garten and got into a conversation with the young man sitting on the stool next to me, who was a recently arrived junior professor in one of the science departments of the university. I told him that I was a book collector, and he told me that he and his wife had just bought a house that had belonged to a deceased history professor and the garage was full of books about Texas, which I could have if I agreed to take all of them.

I followed him home and found that his garage did indeed have lots of books in it, but most of them were badly charred from a fire. The undamaged ones were pamphlets and paper-bound county histories, which had been tied together so tightly in bundles that the fire had not damaged them. I cleaned out his garage for him and put everything in the bed of my Dodge pickup truck, thanked him, and stopped at a dumpster to dispose of the books that were too badly burned to salvage. When I got home I found that I had about two dozen readable books with charred covers and about three hundred pamphlets, offprints, and paper-bound county histories. I deduced from the fact that some of the county histories were inscribed by their authors to H. Bailey Carroll, a professor of history at UT who wrote a bibliography of Texas county histories, that the books had been part of Carroll's library, which had been destroyed by fire in the early 1960s. Carroll had died in 1966.

The pamphlets were a treasure trove of Texas individualism. There were several Dobie Christmas cards and twenty copies of a four-page circular entitled "The Archives Wars of Texas," which Dobie wrote in 1957 advocating the passage through the legislature of a bill appropriating funds for a State Library and Archives building east of the State Capitol. There was a 126-page wrapper-bound book entitled *Texas Merry Go Round* denouncing a gaggle of Texas politicians of the 1920s, from Governors Ross Sterling and Dan Moody to J. Waddy Tate, the Hot Dog Mayor of Dallas. The book was published by the Sun Publishing Company of Houston in 1933, but no author's name appears on the cover or title page. A tipped-in slip of paper between pages 18 and 19, however, bears the typewritten words, "The Texas Merry Go Round was written by JIMMIE WELCH, a former member of the Department of History of the University of Texas." There was a copy of a pamphlet called *Hounds and Men*, a paean to wolf hunting by a Methodist minister named Philip Whitman Walker, published in Denton in 1950. My favorite was a 1933 pamphlet by Don Biggers entitled *Our Sacred Monkeys Or 20 Years of Jim and Other Jams*, 104 pages outlining the sins of Governor Jim Ferguson. The authors of these pamphlets, and dozens of others in the collection, cared enough about their opinions to pay someone to publish them, and they did not hold back the Tabasco in expressing them.

This windfall stimulated my interest in the back roads and dark corners of Texana, and I started to acquire newly published town, county, and church histories and to look for older ones in used bookstores and antique shops. I was lucky enough to find a nearly perfect copy of F. Lotto's *Fayette County: Her History and Her People*, published in Schulenburg in 1902 by the Schulenburg Sticker Steam Press, in a San Antonio antique shop for two dollars, but I was never able to locate a mimeographed county history that Ben Pingenot told me about, which he claimed bore the title *A History of Zavala County When I Completed This I Did Not Have Enough for a Whole Book So I Added My Uncle John's Account of His Trip to Mexico in 1946.*

About the time that I acquired the F. Lotto history of *Fayette County* I moved from Austin to Round Top in Fayette County to become the curator of the University of Texas's Winedale Historical Center and discovered a new genre of Texas pamphlets: Texas-German family histories. Fayette County had a large Texas-German population, people whose ancestors had come from Germany in the 1840s and 1850s, and many of them belonged to family associations that held regular reunions and published family histories. The oldest and largest of these was the Familia Sack, which encompassed the Von Roeder, Kleberg, Eckhardt, Ploeger, Jessen, and Sterzing families, and published a genealogy called *The Silver Book* every ten years, supplemented by an annual publication called *The Dove*. But there were also the Rombergs, the von Rosenbergs (who not only published a family history but had a family anthem), the Mackensens, the Bauers, the Giesekes, and a host of others. All of these family histories contain valuable information about German immigration to Texas and the customs of Texas German families, and they are rare because they were usually printed in editions of five hundred or one thousand copies and distributed only to family members. Most of them are in English. The epitome of the genre is probably the Jordan family history, *Ernst and Lisette Jordan, German Pioneers in Texas,* written by University of Texas cultural geographer Terry Jordan and his father, Gilbert Jordan, and published by the Von Boeckmann-Jones Company in Austin in 1971. These family histories led me to an interest in the literature of Texas Germans in general, and I have several shelves of memoirs and town and county histories as well as a few literary productions, some in German, but all published in Texas.

In the 1970s I also developed an interest in book design, largely through a friendship with Bill and Sally Wittliff, who had started the Encino Press in Austin in 1964, and Fred and Barbara Whitehead, who had a book design firm in Austin. With the advice of Al Lowman I started collecting books from Texas fine printers, and managed to acquire most of the Encino Press publications and a few Carl Hertzog items, as well as a copy of Lowman's own *This Bitterly Beautiful Land,* a collection of quotations about Texas illustrated by Barbara Whitehead and printed by Bill Holman on a hand press in 1972 in an edition of 275 copies. I think it is the most beautiful book ever produced in Texas. That same year I asked the Whiteheads to design a woodblock print Christmas card for me, which I intended to print myself on Holman's hand press. I planned to send out about two hundred cards. I took the block to Holman's studio, and he showed me how to set up and ink the press. It had a wheel on the side that you had to turn, taking about four steps forward with each impression. After fifteen minutes or so of turning the wheel, Holman asked, "Does your back hurt right here?" putting his hand on the small of his back. When I said that it did, he said, “That means you’ve done about twenty-five copies. When you’ve done fifty it will hurt all up and down your spine.” I mentally made a drastic cut in my Christmas card list, and I believe I finally turned out about eighty cards.

In 1974 Barbara Whitehead designed my first publication, a pamphlet entitled *Texas Germans: A Short Bibliography,* whose cover incorporated a wonderful photograph from the 1890s of two residents of La Grange smoking long German pipes. It was published by the Winedale Historical Center and sold to visitors at the museum bookstore. Two years later, in 1976, I retained Whitehead to design and illustrate with her woodcuts a more ambitious publication for Winedale, a translation by Anders Saustrup of William Trenckmann’s essay “Eine Weihnachtsfeier in trüber Zeit,” a memoir of Christmas in Trenckmann’s German-speaking home in Millheim, Texas, in 1863, first published in Trenckmann’s paper, the *Bellville Wochenblatt,* in 1893. Saustrup, who was married to Trenckmann’s granddaughter, gave the pamphlet the title *Christmas in Troubled Times.* We printed one thousand copies and sent one to every member of the Friends of Winedale. That is my contribution to the pamphlet literature of Texas.

My collecting of Texana waned when I moved to Santa Fe in 1980 and then to Washington, DC, in 1984, although Nick Potter in Santa Fe occasionally called my attention to some choice Texas items in his wonderful shop on Palace Avenue. In Washington I occasionally visited Larry McMurtry’s Booked Up in Georgetown, but there were no bargains there. I did occasionally pick up some Texas bargains on visits to London, which leads me to believe that the best place to buy Texana is as far away from Texas as possible. Since retiring in 2002 and moving to Fort Davis, Texas (population 1,160), I have relied largely on Amazon to fulfill my book needs, although Jean Hardy-Pittman runs an excellent book store in nearby Alpine, Front Street Books, which occasionally has some fine items of Texana on its used book shelves.

The essays in this book are not book reviews. They originated as recommendations to the readers of my weekly column in the *Marfa Big Bend Sentinel*, "The Rambling Boy," of books that I thought they might enjoy, or as discussions in that column of Texas authors that I thought worth calling their attention to. You will find no biting criticism or sarcasm here; I have saved that for my reviews in academic journals, where it has made me a few enemies. I have been writing "The Rambling Boy" for the *Sentinel* since 2004, and I would like to thank the publishers, Robert and Rosario Halpern, for permitting me to reprint these in somewhat expanded form. I hope that my wider circle of readers enjoys them.

Lonn Taylor
Fort Davis, Texas
March 2, 2018

I.
GIANTS AND OLD-TIMERS

JOHN GRAVES

✣ 1 ✣

MYSELF AND STRANGERS

John Graves, *Myself and Strangers.*
New York: Alfred A. Knopf, 2004.

FOR ME, the quintessential Texas writer is not J. Frank Dobie or Walter Prescott Webb or Roy Bedicheck or Larry McMurtry or any of the group of Fort Worth sports writers and pranksters who published in *Texas Monthly* in the 1970s and 1980s. It is John Graves, whose work I have admired and envied since the publication of his first book, *Goodbye to a River,* in 1960. I was a senior at Texas Christian University that year, and Graves's book was about country that I had explored on picnics and Saturday drives—the Brazos Valley west of Fort Worth, where it cuts through the West Cross Timbers—although in reading the book I discovered that my superficial knowledge of it could not compare with Graves's, nor could I ever hope to write about it so lucidly. But the book touched familiar chords, not only because I had seen some of the places described but because what Graves had to say about them transcended the places themselves and even Texas and drew on the common humanistic tradition of Western man that I was spending my college years discovering.

Graves taught at TCU, offering a course in creative writing which I did not take but which two of my friends did, and they were his devoted students, enthusiastic about his quiet insights into the craft of writing, the use of language, and the composition of sentences. I used to see him around the campus, a slight, angular-jawed man with salt-and-pepper hair, friendly eyes, and absolutely no pretensions. We became coffee-shop friends, occasionally sharing the same table in the student center. I listened while Graves talked. Unlike some of the other writers and would-be writers I knew, he was not a flamboyant man, and instead of trying to live like or look like Hemingway, he just tried to write as well as Hemingway. He was a private man, and I knew little about him, except that he had been born in Fort Worth, had been a Marine in the Pacific during World War II, and had recently returned to Texas after spending several years in Spain.

After *Goodbye to a River* there was a long time between books. *Hardscrabble*, about a piece of land he owned down near Glen Rose, came out in 1974 and *From a Limestone Ledge* in 1980. Each one was a carefully polished gem. Since then there have been several extended essays, some introductions to other people's books, and a collection of essays and short fiction. The prolific Larry McMurtry is supposed to have said that Graves never published his failures, which I suppose implies that McMurtry has. Now Graves has given us a new book, *Myself and Strangers* (New York: Alfred A. Knopf, 2004), a memoir of his writing apprenticeship in Spain in the 1950s. And it was reading this book that made me realize why Graves is such a good writer and so quintessentially Texan. In one of his essays Graves wrote, "There is a sort of digestive process by which writers take on influence from people and from books, distributing what they can use of it throughout their own dark psyches in cubbyholes and chinks." *Myself and Strangers* describes this digestive process, part of which is Graves's consciousness of being a Texan and a Southerner in cosmopolitan Mallorca in the 1950s and part of which is his choice of reading, from Faulkner and Ford Madox Ford to Virgil and the King James Bible and Samuel Johnson. Who else but a Texan steeped in the Bible could write a sentence describing grass as "that humble, magnificent, green-and-tawny vegetation upon which Nebuchadnezzar in his madness did feed and Texas was largely built"? Listen to this perfectly balanced sentence in *Hardscrabble* describing the cedar choppers who lived in the West Cross Timbers when he moved there: "There was a narrower gamut of things for them to be in that small world, of course, but they tended to make up for it by being what they were far more emphatically than most people these days are anything." That kind of writing can only come from wide reading combined with keen observation.

Graves came back to Texas from Spain with a long autobiographical novel, *A Speckled Horse*, which he never published. Instead, be began looking at and writing about the country around him, and he has never stopped, and he has never published anything trivial. He is a good man writing well. And, at eighty-four, he is traveling to publicize his new book. Go and meet him, even if you have to drive to Austin or San Antonio to do it.

July 15, 2005

John Graves died at his home near Glen Rose, Texas, on July 31, 2013. He was 92 years old.

✣ 2 ✣

LEGENDS OF TEXAS

J. Frank Dobie, *Legends of Texas*. Austin: The Texas Folklore Society, 1924.

It is hard for me to write dispassionately about J. Frank Dobie because the first adult book I ever read was his *Legends of Texas*, which he edited for the Texas Folklore Society in 1924. My grandmother gave it to me when I was seven years old, and I devoured it. It was the first book I had ever read that referred to people I knew about. Dobie's uncle Jim Dobie, whom he refers to several times, once courted my grandmother's little sister. Judge W. P. McLean, who figures in the story about Moro's gold, was a family friend in Fort Worth. That book made the connection between life and literature for me. I moved on to other Dobie books, and my first teenage writing efforts were bad imitations of Dobie's tale-telling.

Although I occasionally saw Dobie on the Drag in Austin during the last years of his life, I never had the courage to walk up to him and introduce myself. By all accounts he was a nice man, although Américo Paredes cruelly parodied him as the patronizing blowhard K. Hank Harvey in *George Washington Gomez*, a novel that Paredes wrote in the late 1930s but that was not published until 1990, long after Dobie's death. Stephen Harrigan paints an unflattering picture of him as Vance Martindale, a callow and ambitious English professor, in his novel *Remembering Ben Clayton*. In his 2009 biography, *J. Frank Dobie: A Liberated Mind*,

Steven L. Davis traces Dobie's intellectual development but says little about his personal life except that in 1919, when his wife, Bertha, was struck with the Spanish influenza, Dobie chose to remain with the army in France, where he was enrolled in the Sorbonne, rather than apply for a transfer home to be with her. Davis quotes a letter that she wrote him but never mailed, saying that he "cares a thousand times more for experience than he does for me." Like most creative people, Dobie was undoubtedly selfish.

If I had to classify Dobie as a writer—and I hate classifications and categories—I would have to put him squarely in the camp of the Regionalists, a group of American writers who flourished in the 1920s, 30s, and 40s, who extolled the virtue of regional differences over mass culture, and rural life over industrialism. They included Willa Cather, William Faulkner, Lewis Mumford, Robert Penn Warren, John Crowe Ransom, Mary Austin, John G. Neihardt, Bernard De Voto, Stanley Vestal, Robert P. T. Coffin, Zora Neale Hurston, Oliver La Farge, and Mari Sandoz. Many had links to the emerging academic study of folklore and drew on material gathered by folklorists; some considered themselves folklorists. A few were utopians, attempting to formulate a culture based on American roots as an alternative to what they perceived as an alien European culture being disseminated from New York. All were anti-modernists, wistfully clinging to an image of an older and apparently simpler America, the "sunny slopes of long ago" that Dobie used to offer toasts to, the "old rock" that his cattlemen heroes were cut from.

But Dobie was different from most of his fellow regionalists. They expressed themselves in fiction, poetry, or, in the case of Mumford, De Voto, and Vestal, essays and historical narratives, often based on folk sources. Dobie, as far as I know, never attempted a novel or wrote a poem. What Dobie excelled in was turning oral narratives into short written pieces. He had an ability to get people to talk, a sharp ear for cadence and language, and an uncanny ability to create a stage for his narrator. Most of his books are in fact strings of finely crafted anecdotes derived from interviews with stove-up cowboys, prospectors, and desert rats.

Dobie's focus on oral tradition stemmed from his conviction that the narratives of old-timers had a value in themselves and did not need to be adapted into fiction or poetry to have communicative power. He saw their unadorned and unmediated words as "truly Homeric" artistic creations that contained truths about the "mind, metaphor, and mores of the common people" that escaped academic historians. He disdained the "PhDs who would write learned historical monographs on 'Utah Carl' and 'Little Joe the Wrangler' that would be full of 'ethnological palaver' and would obscure the experience of hearing the singer or narrator 'vivid and alive.'"

Much of Dobie's popularity stemmed from the fact that he was in the right place at the right time. The oil-rich state of Texas was just beginning to flex its muscles in the early 1930s, preparing for the 1936 centennial celebration by shedding its Confederate southern identity and assuming a new and more dynamic one as part of the cattle kingdom, and Dobie wrote about ranchers and cowboys rather than cotton planters and plantation houses. When the centennial celebration came, Dobie was smack in the middle of it. He served on the Centennial Commission's Advisory Board of Texas Historians, got into a public dispute with the sculptor Pompeo Coppini about the Alamo cenotaph, published *The Flavor of Texas*, and emerged as the state's best-known spokesman, Mr. Texas. When the national spotlight shined on Texas it shined on J. Frank Dobie.

Dobie's reputation declined after his death, reaching its nadir in Larry McMurtry's ill-tempered 1981 denunciation of his books as "a congealed mass of virtually undifferentiated anecdotage; endlessly repetitious, thematically empty, structureless, and carelessly written." I don't think he was as bad as all that. It's true that he never wrote anything to equal Cather's *O, Pioneers!* or Faulkner's *Absalom, Absalom!*, but his books did make Texans with an inherited cultural inferiority complex realize that their native soil was fertile with literary inspiration, and they gave ordinary people a place in history long before "peoples' history" became fashionable. Most of all, he knew a good story when he heard one.

May 12, 2015

3

A VAQUERO OF THE BRUSH COUNTRY (1929)

J. Frank Dobie, *A Vaquero of the Brush Country.* Dallas: The Southwest Press, 1929.

J. FRANK DOBIE, who died in 1964, wrote nineteen books about Texas. Some people say that his first one, *A Vaquero of the Brush Country,* published in 1929, was his best. And some people say he didn't write it.

The book is about cowboying in the chaparral of South Texas in the 1870s and 80s, but it had its genesis in the Big Bend. Dobie came to Alpine in 1910, fresh out of college, to teach high school English. During the year that he lived there he became friends with John Duncan Young, a dealer in land and ranches and the part owner of a marble quarry, a man thirty years Dobie's senior. As a young man Young had worked all over the brush country that Dobie had grown up in and had known ranchers that were friends of Dobie's parents. The two men spent many evenings on the wide porch of Young's house, Young talking and Dobie listening. Among other things, Young told Dobie about his dream of building a ten-story marble hotel in San Antonio, using marble from his quarry, for the use of old trail drivers and cowboys when they came to town.

Young had been both a cowboy and a trail driver. He was born in a log house near Lockhart in 1856, the son of a circuit-riding Baptist preacher who raised horses on the side. He started riding and roping at the age of seven; at twelve he was riding with regular cow outfits; and by the time he finished school at sixteen he was a seasoned vaquero. For the next twenty years Young gathered cattle in the brush country to be driven north to stock new ranges; helped drive those herds north; dodged Comanches on the High Plains; and fought gun battles with Mexican bandits and home-grown cattle thieves. He did about everything a Texas cowboy could do in those years

In 1890 a San Antonio doctor diagnosed Young with tuberculosis, and he moved with his wife and children to the higher Devil's River country, eventually settling in Ozona. There a district judge appointed him receiver of a bankrupt ranch, and he discovered that he had a talent for selling ranches. That became his main business. He moved to Alpine in 1906.

Young had a comfortable income from his real estate business—his commissions and fees from the sale of just two big ranches came to $27,000—but Dobie, in the introduction to *A Vaquero of the Brush Country*, describes him as a dreamer, and he dreamed of ways to get richer. In 1909 he and two South Texas cattlemen, Tom Coleman and D. J. Woodward, bought mineral leases on Marble Mountain, about twenty miles southwest of Alpine, and reopened an old quarry there. Young and his partners spent a small fortune building a road to the quarry, drilling wells in order to get sufficient water, and installing machinery. They claimed that the mountain was solid marble in forty-two colors, ranging from snow white to ebony black, but they could never get the transportation costs of the marble low enough to show a profit, and after fifteen years they sold out to a group of Californians who never made a profit either.

A few years later Young got involved in a project to build a smelter in Alpine to serve operating mines in northern Mexico and potential mines in the Big Bend. The Metal Products Association of Texas bought 570 acres north of Alpine and a trainload of steel and started building a plant, but costs escalated, construction lagged, a lawsuit was filed, and the uncompleted building caught fire and burned to the ground. It was uninsured. Young lost his entire investment.

In 1925, however, Young had an idea that he thought would enable him to build his marble hotel. Western novels and movies had made the cowboy a national hero. Young had been a cowboy. He would write a book about his life that would earn him a fortune. In the summer of 1925 he wrote his friend Dobie, outlining the content of the book and saying, "I'll need somebody to go over the writing and put it into shape." By then Dobie was teaching at the University of Texas and was the secretary of the Texas Folklore Society. He offered to help Young.

The book was four years in the making. Young sent Dobie a series of sparse accounts of his adventures, and Dobie fleshed them out, adding information from his own research, contributing an entire chapter on Anglo-Mexican conflict along the border, and stitching Young's incidents together into a complete narrative. When the book was finally published in 1929, the title page read, "A Vaquero of the Brush Country, By J. Frank Dobie, Partly from the Reminiscences of John Young." This was apparently satisfactory to Young, who nailed a sign over the front door of his Alpine house that said "The Vaquero" and corresponded with Dobie until his death in 1932. His only complaint was that the publisher did not sell enough copies to make him rich.

In 1994, sixty years after Young's death and thirty years after Dobie's, three of Young's great-grandchildren decided that their ancestor had not gotten a fair shake, even though Dobie and Young had split the profits fifty-fifty. In June 1994 they filed a petition in federal district court in Austin demanding that the University of Texas Press, which had acquired the copyright and kept the book in print, give John Young equal status with Dobie as coauthor on the title page of subsequent editions. The court ruled in their favor, and since 1998 the words on the title page have been, “A Vaquero of the Brush Country: The Life and Times of John D. Young, by John D. Young and J. Frank Dobie.”

University of Texas professor Don Graham, who chronicled this authorship dispute in an article in the Fall 2006 issue of *Southwestern American Literature*, feels that the court’s ruling was unjust in light of Dobie’s extensive rewriting of Young’s material and his own substantial original contributions. I agree. It is the only case I know of a sole author being demoted to a secondary coauthor by a federal court.

May 28, 2015

4

A VAQUERO OF THE BRUSH COUNTRY (1998)

John D. Young and J. Frank Dobie,
A Vaquero of the Brush Country:
The Life and Times of John D. Young.
Austin: The University of Texas Press, 1998.

READERS may recall that a few weeks back I wrote a column about J. Frank Dobie and John D. Young of Alpine and the dispute between Young's descendants and the University of Texas Press about the actual authorship of *A Vaquero of the Brush Country*, the book the two men produced together. I said that I thought that Dobie had gotten a raw deal when a Federal court, long after both men's deaths, ruled that Young was the principal coauthor and that his name should appear beside Dobie's on the title page and in fact should be first.

Three weeks ago I was sitting in my study when the phone rang. It was a call from former congressman Duncan Hunter of California, who identified himself as a great-grandson of John Young. He told me that he had read my column and that he had documents that would make me change my mind about the justice of the court's ruling: thirty letters that Dobie wrote to Young while they were working on the book, which Hunter thought proved beyond doubt that Young wrote most of the book. He then started reading me excerpts from the letters over the phone. I suggested to him that if he would send me copies of the letters I would read through them and that if they convinced me to change my mind I would certainly write a column saying so.

Hunter said, "I'm doing better than that, I'm bringing them to you. I'll be in Fort Davis in an hour and a half." It turned out that he was calling from Fort Stockton. He was driving across Texas to his home in San Diego and had decided to take a detour in order to visit me. I gave him directions to our house, and in an hour and a half he was at our front door, a sheaf of papers in his hand.

Congressman Hunter is a handsome, rough-cut man in his late 60s, affable and persuasive in the way that a good trial lawyer is. He sat on our screen porch and talked for an hour, making the case that his great-grandfather was not only the main author of *A Vaquero of the Brush Country* but the man who educated Dobie about nineteenth-century cowboy life, turning him, as Hunter put it, "from a bow-tied schoolteacher into a big-hatted expert on cattle and cowboy life." To prove this point he read aloud passages from Dobie's letters to Young that were long lists of questions about the details of working cattle, catching mustangs, and driving herds north. "What was the method for carrying a chunk of fire?" Dobie wrote. "About what date did cattlemen cease to gather annually to make cash settlements with each other?" "How about some reminiscences on old time cowboy dances?" and so on for page after page. Young's answers are not among the papers that Hunter left with me, but they are in the book.

Congressman Hunter's letters are the kind that collaborators write to each other, and they convinced me that Young was a coauthor of the book and deserved to have his name with Dobie's on the title page, but they did not convince me that he was the principal author. They do show that the young Dobie was a skilled flatterer. "I am convinced that you are on the eve of getting out the best cowboy book ever written," Dobie wrote to Young at the beginning of the project. About a word image of Young's in Chapter 20 Dobie wrote, "The picture of that Mexican with the iron hand picking up red hot coals stays with me and will stay with me as long as I live." On the receipt of a new chapter from Young, he wrote, "I do not believe anything is better than this. This is THE STUFF."

In addition, the letters reveal an unpleasantly egotistical and grasping side of Dobie. At the beginning of the project, in December 1925, Dobie wrote Young, "I want it clearly understood that I am not interested in this matter for the money there may be in it. Absolutely I do not want a cent for my work, would not take a cent." Young, however, insisted on making Dobie a fifty-fifty partner in the enterprise, and in February 1927 the two men drew up a contract specifying that they would split the royalties that way. In February 1928, however, Dobie, now an adjunct professor at the University of Texas and secretary of the Texas Folklore Society, wrote to Young saying that "in view of the great amount of work I was adding to the book and the added prestige I was attaining, I thought I should have a more favorable contract." He sent Young an amended contact which granted Dobie 100 percent of all royalties up to $500, after which the fifty-fifty split would become effective, and in addition gave Dobie all of the magazine and newspaper rights. Young acquiesced and signed the new contract. After the book was published, in October, 1930, Dobie offered to buy all of Young's rights for $600, and Young declined. Ten years later, when the book was about to be reprinted by Little, Brown, he offered Young's destitute widow $50 for the same rights.

Oddly enough, the letters that Congressman Hunter brought me to prove that Young wrote most of *A Vaquero of the Brush Country* are the same letters that Professor Don Graham at the University of Texas used to argue, in an article in the Fall 2014 issue of *Southwestern American Literature,* that Dobie was the true author of the book. They are in the Dobie Papers at the Harry Ransom Center in Austin. If they prove anything, they prove that two people can look at the same evidence and draw completely opposing conclusions. What would prove that Young was the true author of the book would be a comparison of the manuscript that Young sent Dobie with the published text, and unfortunately that complete manuscript has never turned up. Until it does, I am withdrawing from this controversy.

July 23, 2015

✣ 5 ✣

WITH HIS PISTOL IN HIS HAND

Américo Paredes, *With His Pistol in His Hand.*
Austin: University of Texas Press, 1958.

THIS CINCO DE MAYO is the 151st anniversary of the Battle of Puebla, in which a Mexican army led by Texas-born General Ignacio Zaragoza defeated an army of French invaders. It is also the fourteenth anniversary of the death of Américo Paredes, a Texan who fought *con su pluma en su mano,* in the words of Tish Hinojosa's song about him, for the recognition of Mexican-American culture in Texas.

Don Américo, as his students and colleagues called him in his later years, was a professor of English and anthropology at the University of Texas at Austin for forty-one years, from 1958 until his death in 1999. He started his career there with an explosion and made noises on the campus throughout most of his academic career. The explosion was the publication of his doctoral dissertation, *With His Pistol in His Hand: A Border Ballad and Its Hero,* by the University of Texas Press in 1958. The book is a scholarly study of a 1901 incident in Karnes County, Texas, in which a farm hand named Gregorio Cortez killed a sheriff who was trying to arrest him and then led dozens of posses on a ten-day, 500-mile horseback chase across South Texas before he was finally captured. The incident gave rise to a *corrido,* a ballad, in which Cortez is portrayed as a hero persecuted by Anglo-Americans, and Paredes's book dealt both with the facts of the incident and the structure of the ballad and its many variants. It was an academic approach to an oral tradition, but its publication raised hackles all over Texas because Paredes suggested that there might be another side to the long-accepted accounts of conflict between Anglos and Mexicanos in South Texas. In the book Paredes described the Texas Rangers as instruments of terrorism and questioned the scholarship of two Texas heroes, historian Walter Prescott Webb and folklorist J. Frank Dobie.

In the official University of Texas biography of Paredes the book is described as "an immediate and outstanding success." The fact is that when it first appeared, *With His Pistol in His Hand* was savaged by the Texas historical establishment. In a review in the *Southwestern Historical Quarterly* Roy Sylvan Dunn, a professor of history at Texas Tech and a former Texas State Librarian, described it as "slanted" and "distorted," "an attempt to pass off imaginative subjectivities as absolute truth," and the work of "a person who is careless." Nor did it receive universal popular acclaim on publication. A former Texas Ranger called the University of Texas Press office to say that he wanted "to pistol-whip the son-of-a-bitch who wrote that book." It was only later, with the rise of the Chicano movement, that *With His Pistol in His Hand* was recognized as a seminal work of scholarship and the foundational text of the Chicano movement in Texas.

Paredes did not start out in life to be an academic. He was a child of the border, born in Brownsville, Texas, in 1915, the son of parents who had moved across the border from Matamoros in 1904. He spent the summers of his childhood across the river on an uncle's ranch, listening to the old men tell stories and sing corridos around a campfire. As a young man he wanted to be a singer and a poet. He contributed essays to the *Brownsville Herald*, and a local print shop published his first book of poems, *Cantos de*

Adolescensia, when he was twenty-one. He played the guitar, hung around bars in Brownsville and Matamoros with a Bohemian crowd, and drafted a novel about the border titled *George Washington Gomez*.

World War II changed Paredes's life. He volunteered for the army and was eventually sent to Japan. He took his discharge there in 1946 and stayed in Asia four more years, working as a public relations officer for the Red Cross in Japan, China, and Korea. During those years he met his wife, Amelia Sidzu Nagamine, the daughter of a Japanese diplomat and a Uruguayan mother, who also worked for the Red Cross. They married in Tokyo in 1948, and celebrated their fiftieth anniversary the year before Paredes's death.

The Paredeses returned to the US in 1950, and Paredes, now sure of what he wanted to become, enrolled in the University of Texas. He got his PhD in 1958. For his dissertation topic he chose one of the corridos he had learned as a young man, *El Corrido de Gregorio Cortez*. Stith Thompson, one of the founders of the discipline of folklore in the United States, was a visiting professor at the University of Texas that year and was so impressed with Paredes's dissertation that he urged the University of Texas Press to publish it. The press tried to persuade Paredes to tone down his criticism of the Texas Rangers and of Walter Prescott Webb, whose 1935 book, *The Texas Rangers*, had contributed to the Rangers' heroic legend, but Paredes stood his ground, and the book was published as Paredes wrote it.

In 1958 Paredes became an assistant professor of English at the University of Texas, one of the few Mexican Americans on the faculty. He was a mentor to the increasing number of Chicano students, and in the mid-1960s he spearheaded a controversial movement to create an interdisciplinary Mexican American Studies program at the university. The university's administration at first agreed, and established a Center for Mexican American Studies with Paredes as director, but then backpedaled and refused to implement a corresponding degree program. Paredes resigned as director three times between 1970 and 1972 before the program was fully in place. Today the Center for Mexican American Studies is one of the flagship programs of the university, with sixty associated faculty members.

Paredes went on to publish many other significant books and articles in the field of folklore. He was a familiar figure on the University of Texas campus for many years, a slight man with horn-rimmed glasses and a short white beard, frequently dressed in a white guayabera and a Panama hat. Tish Hinojosa sings about him that *con su pluma en su mano / con paciencia y sin temor / escribió muchas verdades / y respeto nos ganó* (with his pen in his hand / patiently and fearlessly / he wrote the truth / and gained us respect). This Cinco de Mayo, let's honor not only Ignacio Zaragoza but Américo Paredes, a fighter with pen and paper.

May 2, 2013

✣ 6 ✣

THE LAST PICTURE SHOW

Larry McMurtry, *The Last Picture Show.*
New York: Dial Press, 1966.

I WAS A SENIOR at Texas Christian University in 1960 when Larry McMurtry's first novel, *Horseman Pass* By, came out. A longtime member of the English faculty, Miss Mable Major, tried to make sure that no innocent undergraduate eyes were ever sullied by the improper words in the book's text by checking it out of the Texas Christian University library on extended loan and keeping it checked out until she retired. If you wanted to read it you had to buy it at the bookstore across the street from the campus.

Although McMurtry is revered among Texans for his heroic 1985 novel about a nineteenth-century cattle drive, *Lonesome Dove*—I know people who have named cats and dogs after the two protagonists, Gus McCrae and Woodrow Call, and I also know a prominent collector of Texana who compares the book to the Iliad and the Odyssey—for my money his early novels about contemporary Texans are his best: *Leaving Cheyenne, The Last Picture Show,* and the trilogy made up of *Moving On, All My Friends Are Going to Be Strangers,* and *Terms of Endearment.* Of these, *The Last Picture Show* is my absolute favorite. I know of no other novel that captures the sweetness and pain of being an adolescent in a small Texas town, or indeed anywhere, so perfectly. I remember when it was published in 1967 Dave Hickey pronounced McMurtry a

LARRY McMURTRY

genius for being able to write convincingly about adolescent characters when adolescents, by definition, have not yet formed their characters.

Not everyone was enthusiastic about it. When the movie was being filmed in McMurtry's home town of Archer City in 1971, there were letters written to the local newspaper denouncing it as "a dirty book" and "trash" due to McMurtry's portrayals of adolescent sexual activity. McMurtry himself, in an article in *Holiday Magazine* about driving around the perimeter of Texas, told about a cashier in an El Paso café who, having identified him by the name on his credit card, said, "Oh, you're the man who wrote that book about all them naked people up in Wichita Falls," referring to the swimming party sequence at the rich boy's house in Wichita Falls.

McMurtry set the novel in the fictional town of Thalia, Texas, named after the muse of comedy and a thinly disguised version of his own hometown of Archer City (population 2,000). Peter Bogdanovich's movie version was filmed in Archer City, and I once drove a lady from New York two hundred miles out of the way in an ice storm because she had seen the movie and wanted to see Archer City. She said it looked just like it did in the movie.

For those of you who have not seen the movie or read the book, *The Last Picture Show* is the story of three high school kids, Sonny Crawford and Duane Moore and Jacy Farrow, the girl both boys aspire to, coming of age in the early 1950s in a dying West Texas town. While Sonny and Duane are beautifully delineated, and there is a supporting cast of neatly-drawn characters both comic and sad, McMurtry's masterpiece is Jacy Farrow, a spoiled unhappy rich girl who is discovering how to use her sexuality to manipulate people. Unfortunately, most of us have known someone like her.

The power of the novel lies in the fact that McMurtry has localized a universal story and has done it with such a finely pointed pen that we feel that we have known not just Jacy but all of his characters all of our lives. The leading character is the town of Thalia itself, a dusty, windswept, decaying West Texas county seat where the picture show, the pool hall, and the cafe are the only going places in town. We have all been there, or at least been through there. It could be somewhere between Wichita Falls and Lubbock, but it could also be Winesburg, Ohio, or Gopher Prairie, Minnesota, or one of Chekhov's garrison towns on the steppes of Russia. It is a place everyone with any sensitivity or ambition wants to get out of.

In 1981, after publishing *The Last Picture Show* and his trilogy of novels set in contemporary Houston, McMurtry published an article in the *Texas Observer* in which he chastised Texas writers for following the nineteenth-century frontier themes laid out by J. Frank Dobie and Walter Prescott Webb. He told his readers that the future of Texas writing lay in contemporary urban themes, saying that the cowboy myth was finally dead and there was no more to be said about it. Then he went on to write *Lonesome Dove* and any number of other novels set in the nineteenth-century West. But I have always felt that his heart was not in them to the extent that it was in those early novels, and that perhaps he should have followed his own advice.

The Last Picture Show has generated a bibliography of its own. McMurtry wrote three sequels to it, tracing Duane Moore's progress through adulthood: *Texasville, Duane's Depressed,* and *When the Light Goes.* In 1997 an Archer City girl named Ceil Cleveland, who thought herself to be the principal model for Jacy Farrow, published a memoir called *Whatever Happened to Jacy Farrow?* Several academics have produced thorny essays on the deeper meaning of the book, and Grover Lewis published a fine piece in *Rolling Stone* about the filming of the movie in Archer City. But the best critique I have ever heard of it was voiced by a young man I knew in Round Top, Texas (population 70), in the

1970s, a man I'll call Stuart. Stuart was a lay-about in his late twenties who had some sort of unsupervised job with the telephone company that allowed him to spend his afternoons hanging around country bars drinking beer and shooting pool. One afternoon I encountered him sitting at a table with several empty beer bottles on it, holding open a book and crying great big tears which were splashing down on its pages. "Stuart, what in the world is the matter?" I said. "It's this book," he said, holding up a copy of *The Last Picture Show*. "It's about me. It's the only book I've ever read that was about me."

I've always wanted to pass that story on to McMurtry. I think he'd like it.

October 30, 2008

7

A PERSONAL COUNTRY

A. C. Greene, *A Personal Country.*
New York: Alfred A. Knopf, 1969.

WRITERS are generally pretty interesting people, and I have been fortunate in knowing quite a few. By far the most interesting, and also the luckiest, was A. C. Greene, who died in 2002 at the age of seventy-nine. I say the luckiest because of something that happened to A. C. shortly before I met him. A. C. was a journalist, and in the early 1960s he was the book page editor for the *Dallas Times-Herald.* The book page was in the Sunday paper, and every Monday morning an elderly lady named Lula Gooch would call A. C. and tell him how much she had enjoyed that week's book page. A. C. vaguely knew that Gooch was related to the family that owned the paper, but he never met her or laid eyes on her. When Lula Gooch died in 1965, she left A. C. her shares of stock in the *Times-Herald*, which amounted to 20 percent of the total number of shares. The shares had never been publicly traded, and no one knew how much they were worth; they had been very tightly held within the Gooch family. A year later the *Times-Herald* was sold to the *Los Angeles Times* for $72 million. A. C., who had probably never earned more than $15,000 a year in his life and was supporting a wife and three children, was suddenly a millionaire.

He quit his job at the *Times-Herald*, bought his wife a mink coat and himself a Lincoln Continental sedan, and applied for and won a Texas Institute of Letters Dobie-Paisano fellowship for a six-month writing residency at J. Frank Dobie's Paisano Ranch outside of Austin. There A. C. completed his first, and, in my opinion, his best book *A Personal Country* (Alfred A. Knopf, 1969).

A Personal Country is about the part of Texas that lies west of the Brazos and east of the Pecos, and it is a mixture of reminiscence, history, and old folks' tales that A. C. heard as a boy. A. C. grew up in Abilene, where his grandmother Maude E. Cole was the head librarian at the Carnegie Public Library, and he credits her with fostering his early interest in books and writing. One of his great-grandmothers, as a young widow of twenty-eight with three children, had married a seventy-three-year old veteran of the Texas Revolution who had been awarded a land grant for his military service and was thought to be wealthy, an appropriate protector for a young widow. She outlived him by many years to become the last surviving widow of a Texas revolutionary soldier, drawing a pension of twelve dollars a month from the State of Texas. A. C. remembered her sitting in her living room, saying, "Lord, I know that you will make my enemies my footstool, but when, Lord, when?" A. C. drew on these memories, and on the local histories his grandmother Cole introduced him to, to create a book that, in my opinion, ranks right up there with John Graves's *Goodbye to a River* as a Texas classic.

I first met A. C. in Austin in 1969. He had just completed his Dobie-Paisano fellowship and I had my first real writing job, producing entries for the *Supplement* to the old two-volume *Handbook of Texas* for the Texas State Historical Association. We had both signed up for a University of Texas course in historic preservation, taught by preservation architect Wayne Bell, and we spent nearly every weekend that spring together on field trips to San Antonio, Rio Grande City, Galveston, Round Top, and other places that were unfamiliar to us. Even though A. C. was nearly twenty years my senior, we bonded because we knew the same country, the stretch of West Texas between Fort Worth and Abilene. A. C. proposed to his wife in the same all-night café in Weatherford that I used to take girls to for coffee and pie on late-night drives when I was in college at TCU. We shared an enthusiasm for Texas's Victorian courthouses, and could spend hours comparing the ones at Decatur, Albany, Weatherford, and Granbury. We even knew some of the same stories, including the whole cycle of tales that clustered around Granbury lawyer "Bull" Durham, a Rhodes scholar who argued cases in court barefoot. A. C. was a superb storyteller, and he had a lot of adventures to draw on—he had been a Marine in China at the end of World War II—but unlike many good storytellers he was also a good listener, and he not only listened to my stories but urged me to write them down. He was my first writing mentor, and the kindest and best critic I have ever known. He showed me that almost anything can be improved with more work and the use of a dictionary.

A. C. went on to write twenty more books, including one about following the Butterfield Overland Trail across West Texas; histories of Austin and Dallas; and the controversial *50 Best Books About Texas* (the publisher, Anne Dickson, added an entry on *A Personal Country*, written by A. C.'s old friend Bill Porterfield, without A. C.'s knowledge). But none of his later books equaled the immediacy and poignancy of *A Personal Country*.

A. C. maintained a love-hate relationship with Dallas. He had many friends there, and he was a frequent commentator on KERA's pioneering program "Newsroom," but he hated the city's pretension and boosterism. In 1992, when developer Trammel Crow persuaded the city fathers to spend $9 million on a 4.2 acre sculpture composed of forty-nine larger-than-life bronze Longhorn steers and three bronze cowboys in order to publicize Dallas's alleged western heritage, A. C.'s acerbic comment was that it would be more accurate if it portrayed forty-nine insurance salesmen. By then he had moved to the idyllic village of Salado, between Waco and Austin.

I moved away from Texas, first to New Mexico and then to Washington, DC, and I did not see A. C. for fifteen years. But in the mid-1990s I was invited to come from Washington to Denton, Texas, to give an illustrated lecture on a book I had written about the evolution of the popular image of the cowboy. To my surprise and delight A. C. was in the audience. He had driven 175 miles from Salado to Denton to hear me. After the lecture he took me aside and congratulated me, telling me that I had something to say that no one had ever said before, and then he showed me how I could have made more effective use of one of the images I had shown. As I said, A. C. was the best and kindest of critics.

March 1, 2018

✣ 8 ✣

I'LL DIE BEFORE I'LL RUN

C. L. Sonnichsen, *I'll Die Before I'll Run: The Story of the Great Feuds of Texas.* New York: Harper, 1951.

I OWE MY FIRST appearance in scholarly print to Dr. C. L. Sonnichsen, professor of English at what is now the University of Texas at El Paso and one of Texas's most prolific folklorists. In 1951 Sonnichsen published a book called *I'll Die Before I'll Run: The Story of the Great Feuds of Texas.* One of my father's cousins sent our family a copy, with a note on the flyleaf that said, "Sounds like the author talked to the other side of our feud." I was eleven years old, and I did not know that our family had a feud. I asked my father about it, and he suggested that I read the book. I did, and in the chapter called "Bullets for Uncle Buck's Boys" I learned that my grandmother Taylor's uncles and first cousins in San Augustine, Texas, had been involved in a feud in the early 1900s that had resulted in several killings, including that of my grandmother's first cousin Curg Border. Sonnichsen described Curg as "a pretty bad sort," and his text was accompanied by a drawing by José Cisneros showing him as a sullen-looking fellow with a rat tail moustache gripping the bars of a jail cell. Sonnichsen had made a minor error in recounting the Border genealogy, confusing two generations of Curg Border's forebears, and being a somewhat priggish eleven-year-old I sat down and wrote him a letter, telling him where he had gone wrong and citing entries from the Border family Bible as evidence. Sonnichsen wrote a very polite reply, thanking me for correcting him and promising to remedy the error in the next edition of the book. Sure enough, when the 1962 edition came out, footnote two for Chapter Thirteen says, "Lonn W. Taylor of Manila, P.I. set me straight on William Border." I was proud as punch.

I regret that I never met Sonnichsen so that I could thank him in person. He taught at the University of Texas at El Paso from 1931 to 1972 and then moved to Tucson, where he continued to write books until his death at eighty-nine in 1991. He produced eighteen books on Western history, all of them meticulously researched and beautifully written.

Sonnichsen liked to describe himself as a *historianus herbidus*, which he translated as "grassroots historian." He got his PhD at Harvard in seventeenth- and eighteenth-century English literature, and those were the subjects that he expected to teach when he arrived in El Paso in 1931, but the president of the College of Mines (as UTEP was then known), John Barry, had other ideas and assigned him to teach a new course on Southwestern life and literature, modeled on the course that J. Frank Dobie had recently instituted at the University of Texas. Sonnichsen gulped and accepted the assignment. It became the most popular course on campus, and "Doc" Sonnichsen the most popular professor. He never looked back.

As a professor, Sonnichsen was expected to write something. He had come to El Paso intending to write a biography of the eighteenth-century English poet Samuel Butler, but his new course changed his focus. He was rooming in the home of an El Paso insurance man named Belk, and Belk told him stories about a feud in Richmond, Texas, in the 1890s between two political factions who called themselves the Jaybirds and the Woodpeckers. Sonnichsen, intrigued by the names of the factions, decided to write about the feud, and in the summer of 1933 he spent a month in Richmond researching it. It was there that he first developed the techniques that he refined into what he called grassroots history: a combination of interviews with old-timers; examinations of newspaper files; and research in courthouse records.

Sonnichsen was a genius at getting close-mouthed people to talk about subjects that were distasteful to them. He once described his interview technique as "conversational dentistry, every fact wrenched out by its roots." Sonnichsen was probably such a good oral historian because he was a good listener. He had an ear for the telling phrase and the revealing story. In *Cowboys and Cattle Kings*, a book he wrote by driving a 1941 Packard fifteen thousand miles across thirteen states and listening to ranch people and cowboys talk, he quotes a cowboy declining a bowl of after-dinner Jell-O: "I'd as soon ride into a west wind with a funnel in my mouth." He liked to say that in his *Roy Bean: Law West of the Pecos*, he told every Roy Bean story there was except one, which he heard at a signing party in San Angelo after the book was published. "A man got mixed up with a girl in the red light district down in Langtry," Sonnichsen said, "and she killed him. Bean was called in as coroner and viewed the corpse, emerging with the verdict of suicide. A visiting lawyer in town said, 'Roy, this man was obviously murdered. You can't say he committed suicide.' Bean answered, 'I told him if he played around with that girl he was committing suicide and by God be did!'"

Sonnichsen was an observer as well as a listener, and a master of descriptive prose. Here is his delineation of Charley Cocanower, a hitchhiker he picked up just north of Seymour, Texas, when he was working on *Cowboys and Cattle Kings*: "He was one of the most weatherbeaten specimens that ever came out of the brush—an old man bundled in decayed sweaters and defended feebly by a pair of overalls that were in truth on their last legs. About three days' growth of white whiskers waved gently over his furrowed features; a set of fine mahogany teeth peeped out from behind cracked lips; rheumy old eyes lurked behind his steel-rimmed spectacles; and a hat that had known no rest or mercy for many years, high of crown, wavy of brim, and stained with unnamable stains, was jammed down on his head."

Maybe the reason that Sonnichsen was such a good writer was that he tried not to write like an academic—"historical brickmaking, piling facts upon facts like bricks," he called it. "I don't like to write too seriously," he said. "I like to poke a little fun now and then. If there is a chance to raise an eyebrow or put tongue in cheek, that tickles me."

I will always wish I had driven to El Paso to meet him.

October 26, 2017

✣ 9 ✣

PELELIU LANDING

Tom Lea, *Peleliu Landing.* El Paso: C. Hertzog, 1945

FEW AMERICAN cities have embraced a native writer and artist in the way that El Paso has Tom Lea. Usually creative people, like prophets, are without honor in their own country, especially in Texas, where, until recently, artists and writers were considered dangerous weirdos, and people like Robert Rauschenberg and Terry Southern (natives of Port Arthur and Alvarado, respectively) had to go to New York to get any respect. Lea, who was born in El Paso in 1907 and died there in 2001, did leave home for a while as a young man and again during World War II, but the most productive years of his career were spent in El Paso, and El Paso rewarded him with honors. In 1957, at the height of his career, he was named The First Citizen of El Paso at a banquet held in connection with an exhibition of his work and the publication of his two-volume history of the King Ranch. In 1968 the El Paso Public Library named its special collections room after him, and a few years later the El Paso Museum of Art created a Tom Lea Gallery. Now the Tom Lea Institute in El Paso is about to devote a full month to lectures and programs about his life and work. Can you imagine that happening in Dallas? Or Houston?

This hometown veneration may be due to the fact that Lea was not only an accomplished muralist, painter, and illustrator but also a writer of considerable skill, talents that are not usually combined

TOM LEA

in a single individual. Lea did not begin writing until he was nearly forty, and he was jolted into it by a wartime experience, the bloody battle of Peleliu Island in the Pacific. Lea spent World War II as a combat artist for *LIFE* magazine, and when the Seventh Marine Regiment hit the beach at Peleliu he was with them. He spent thirty-two hours under fire before withdrawing to a ship offshore to record what he had seen. He later wrote, "On the beach I found it impossible to do any sketching or writing; my work there consisted of trying to keep from getting killed and trying to memorize what I saw and felt under fire." One of things he memorized was the look on the face of a Marine who was under fire with him, which he immortalized in the painting that he called, "The 2,000–Yard Stare," one of the iconic images of the war. But he also wrote, "before my hand steadied," he said, the essay that became his first book, *Peleliu Landing*, printed in an edition of five hundred copies by Carl Hertzog in 1945. Lea later described that book as "not a page from a history book, not an account of a battle. It is a simple narrative of an experience in battle; like combat itself such a narrative is bound to be personal, confused, benumbed, and in its deepest sense lonely."

Lea went on to write four fine novels and a two-volume history of the King Ranch. All of his novels were "simple narratives," but he labored much harder over them than he did his paintings. He wrote in longhand, standing at a desk, with a blunt pencil. Writing did not come easily to him. He could spend a day on a single paragraph. Lea tried to write as he painted, producing work that was true to his own inner experience of the world. He worked so hard at writing because he was passionate about tapping into that experience and getting it down right.

Passion might seem to be a strange word to describe Lea, who was a short, quiet, introspective man who abhorred flamboyance, artiness, art colonies, and talking about art. But he was passionate. He married his first wife, Nancy Taylor, when they were both nineteen and art students in Chicago. She died from appendicitis ten years later, and the next year he met Sarah Dighton Beane, a young divorcee who was visiting friends in El Paso. They courted for exactly thirty-six hours before Lea proposed to her, and she considered the matter for twenty-four more hours before accepting. They were together for sixty-three years before death ended the marriage.

My favorite Tom Lea painting is a portrait of Sarah, called *Sarah in the Summertime*. Sarah is standing, her hands at her sides, wearing a light summer dress, with the sunlight and the Franklin Mountains behind her. That portrait, like Lea's writing, grew out of the war. Lea carried a photograph of Sarah in that pose, taken in their backyard at 1520 Reynolds Boulevard, in his wallet all through the war. When he came home, the first painting he started was a life-sized rendition of that photograph. He posed Sarah in the same spot in the backyard and made a five-foot seven-inch high sketch of her on butcher paper, which he transferred to canvas. The painting was an act of love, done slowly and without haste. Lea recalled that he worked for twenty-six days painting the flowers on Sarah's dress. It took him two years to finish it, and when it was done he hung it in their living room. Al Lowman, in an essay on Lea, described the painting as "one of the finest love letters ever composed . . . all fresh air and sunshine." It is now in the home of the Leas' son, Dr. James Lea, in Houston.

The lectures and programs about Lea next month are the brainchild of Adair Margo, an El Paso gallery owner who represented Lea in his last years, conducted an oral history project with him, and organized the Tom Lea Institute to perpetuate his memory. The list of events is far too long to reproduce here, but the highlight will be a lecture by Laura Bush, who introduced Lea's work into the White House, at the Plaza Theatre on the evening of October 14. Other programs will cover every conceivable aspect of Lea's life and work. The total menu of more than fifty lectures, exhibitions, film screenings, tours, and seminars can be found at the Institute's website, www.tomlea.net, under "News and Events." If someone in El Paso doesn't know who Tom Lea was by the end of the month, it will be their own fault.

September 27, 2011

✣ 10 ✣

SIX YEARS WITH THE TEXAS RANGERS

James B. Gillett, *Six Years With the Texas Rangers, 1875 to 1881.* Austin: Von Boeckmann-Jones Co., 1921.

Taming the Old West was a young man's job. Most of the men who fought Indians and drove stagecoaches through West Texas in the 1870s were young sprouts in their twenties who had the strength of youth and no sense of their own mortality. But being young in the 1870s meant that many of them survived into the 1930s and 1940s, within the realm of living memory. Men who dodged Comanche lances lived to ride in automobiles and fly in airplanes, to have careers as businessmen and lawyers and bankers, and occasionally to look back in wonder on their youth.

James B. Gillett of Alpine and Marfa was a case in point. Gillett was born in Austin in 1856. He left home to become a cowboy when he was sixteen, and he joined the Texas Rangers a few months before his nineteenth birthday. Many years later he wrote that the day he joined, June 1, 1875, was "the happiest day of my life, for in joining the Rangers I had realized one of my greatest ambitions."

Gillett stayed in the Rangers for six years, and he had enough adventures to last a lifetime. He fought Apaches, Comanches, and outlaws as a member of the Frontier Batallion. He was one of the Rangers who captured the wounded outlaw Sam Bass at Round Rock in 1878, and was with Bass when he died. He chased

Victorio with George Baylor's company of Rangers from Ysleta, and toward the end of his Ranger service he made a mad dash across the Rio Grande with a murderer he had single-handedly arrested on the Mexican side of the river. He did all of this, and a lot more, before he was twenty-five.

Shortly before his thirtieth birthday, Gillett gave up law enforcement and went into the cattle business. He became the foreman of the Gano Brothers G-4 Ranch in southern Brewster County, driving three thousand head of cattle, the foundation of their herd, into the Chisos Basin. He married, and in a few more years he and his wife had their own ranch, the Altuda, south of Alpine. The Alpine papers in the late 1890s and early 1900s are full of stories about James B. Gillett selling yearlings or buying bulls, and about the prize-winning chickens he raised. He became a model of domesticity and fathered six children. He briefly tried his hand at irrigated alfalfa farming in New Mexico, but after a few years he came back to the Big Bend, saying that neither farming nor New Mexico suited him. This time he bought the Barrel Springs Ranch west of Fort Davis and started raising prize Herefords. For the next fifteen years he was totally absorbed in ranching. He became a charter member of the Highland Hereford Breeders' Association and experimented with methods of improving his stock, buying bulls in Kansas City and keeping meticulous breeding records.

But as Gillett approached his mid-sixties, his thoughts turned to his youthful adventures. In 1921 he sat down and wrote his memoirs of those years, a book called *Six Years With the Texas Rangers, 1875 to 1881*, which has become a western classic and is still in print. Writing his memoirs had a mellowing effect on Gillett. Shortly after they were published he turned his ranch over to his son, moved into town, and started collecting frontier relics—guns, saddles, moccasins, Indian pottery. He kept them in a little frame building behind his house, where he loved to sit by the fireplace or on the porch and visit with old Texas Rangers and other friends of his youth who came to Marfa to see him and his collection.

In his book Gillett described some of the stage drivers he had known in the 1870s along the western segment of the San Antonio-El Paso Road, and he said that "there should be a monument erected to the memory of these old stage drivers somewhere along this overland route, for they were the bravest of the brave." In 1935 Gillett himself erected that monument, a bronze plaque that he had cast at his own expense and placed on a huge boulder at Point of Rocks, now a roadside picnic area on Highway 116. The plaque depicts a stagecoach, below which are the words, "Dedicated in memory of Ed Waldy, John M. Dean, August Frenzell, and all other stage drivers who traveled this route, fearless heroes of frontier days. By their courage the West was made." The plaque is still there. It is a monument not only to the stage drivers but to an old man's memories of his youth.

I once met James B. Gillett's grandson, James Evans, at a funeral in Fort Davis. I asked him if he remembered his grandfather, and when he said he did, I asked what he remembered about him. He paused a minute and said, "Well, I remember that he moved his lips when he read the newspaper, and even though I was just a little boy I knew that you weren't supposed to do that."

October 6, 2005

11

O.W. WILLIAMS'S STORIES FROM THE BIG BEND

S. D. Myres (ed.), *O.W. Williams's Stories from the Big Bend.* El Paso: Texas Western College Press, 1965.

A HARVARD LAW SCHOOL graduate with the euphonious name of Oscar Waldo Williams seems like an improbable person to have been an early adventurer in the Big Bend, but in 1901 and 1902 O. W. Williams of Fort Stockton not only walked over most of the country between Lajitas and the Chisos Mountains but wrote and published several little pamphlets about the trip that have become rarities among collectors of Texana. Williams, who was the grandfather of Fort Stockton rancher and oilman Clayton Williams Jr., was born in 1853 and came to Texas from Illinois in 1877. After several surveying trips into the Panhandle and a stint as a prospector and miner in New Mexico, he settled in Fort Stockton and spent the rest of his life there, serving several terms as county judge and practicing his dual professions of lawyer and surveyor almost until his death at ninety-three in 1946. He was both a reader and a writer. He had a large library well stocked with classical literature, he kept diaries, and he carried on a voluminous correspondence. When he reached his mid-sixties he began publishing little paper-bound pamphlets, ranging in length from four to ninety-six pages, containing his observations on his experiences and on the history and natural history of West Texas and New Mexico. He gave these away to his family and friends. No one knows exactly how many of these he wrote. His biographer, S. D. Myres, lists forty separate titles, but there may be more.

In March 1900, Williams was appointed by the county judge of Brewster County to conduct a survey in the southern part of the county in connection with a land title dispute. That job led to several others in the Big Bend, and Williams ended up spending the better part of two years camping with his survey party in the Chisos Mountains and the country around Terlingua and Lajitas. He was, as Myres says, curious about "everything from cactus to Comanches," and he pumped every old-timer he met for information, which he put into his diary and eventually into pamphlets.

Williams published at least seven pamphlets describing his surveying trips in the Big Bend. Three reprinted long letters written to his children in the winter of 1902, and the other four contained stories he had heard in camp. The latter are particularly interesting because Carlysle Graham Raht incorporated them more or less verbatim into his *Romance of the Davis Mountains and the Big Bend Country*, published in 1919, and from there they have found their way into other books and articles about the Big Bend and have become part of the accepted folklore of the region.

Williams's letters show that he was a keen observer, a judicious weigher of evidence, and a well-read scholar. In one he describes the "Smugglers' Trail" from the railroad at Marathon to the Rio Grande (in those days smugglers went from north to south, slipping goods manufactured in the United States into Mexico on muleback in order to avoid paying the Mexican excise tax on them). He says that he was puzzled by what he first thought were wagon tracks, parallel marks in the dust on the trail that varied from five to three feet apart, too close together to have been made by wagon wheels. Enlightenment came when someone explained that they were the result of the Mexican method of moving the pine poles which were cut in the mountains and taken to the river to be used as roof beams. The poles were tied in pairs to horses or mules, one on each side of the saddle, with the ends dragging on the ground behind the animal.

In another letter he relates an encounter with a denizen of Lajitas known as Lying Bill Taylor, who undertook to show Williams a rock shelter full of prehistoric burials near Lajitas. He describes Taylor as "as mild-mannered a man who ever scuttled a ship or cut a throat," an allusion to Byron's poem *Don Juan*, and says, "If he told me any lie, it was not a very big one." He also tells about a visit across the Rio Grande to Don Fermin Flotte, owner of the Matadero Ranch near San Carlos. Flotte was "an old frontiersman of mixed blood," who lived in a fortified structure in which the only way to get animals into the stable was to lead them through the sitting room. Williams describes in great detail the canvas sacks in which water was brought into the Flotte house from the well. The stoppers in the bottom of the sacks were cow horns, inserted with the points outward. The pressure of the water on the hollow insides of the horns held them in place, and the sacks were emptied into water jugs by pressing on the points of the horns.

One member of Williams's survey party was a red-headed native of San Carlos named Natividad Lujan, the grandson of a Spanish soldier at the presidio in San Carlos. Lujan told stories by the campfire at night, and Williams wrote them down and later published them. It is from Lujan that we have the story that Santiago Peak was named after Lujan's uncle Santiago, an Indian fighter from Presidio del Norte who was killed by Apache raiders at its base. Lujan also told Williams the story of Alsate, the chief of the Apaches who lived in the Chisos Mountains. Lujan claimed to have known Alsate as a boy, when the Apaches lived at San Carlos and intermingled with the people there. He told Williams that Alsate's father, who had been stolen by the Apaches as a boy, was the brother of Don Manuel Musquiz, a powerful Chihuahua landowner, and he went on to relate a tale that sounds like something out of Gilbert and Sullivan: about how Alsate's father had a sixth toe on his right foot, which resulted in Alsate being freed from captivity through Musquiz's good offices. Lujan also provided Williams with information about the Comanche chief Bajo El Sol, the bandit El Guero Carranza, and other Big Bend figures who have passed into history, or at least folklore, via Williams's pamphlets.

One of O. W. Williams's children, Clayton Wheat Williams, inherited his father's desire to record and inform and published a three-volume history of West Texas entitled *Never Again* in 1969, and in 1982 a history of Fort Stockton and the trans-Pecos region up to 1895. Clayton Williams Jr. has not yet set pen to paper for publication, although I just received a notice about the release of his biography by Texas writer Mike Cochran by Texas A&M Press, so at least he is carrying on the family tradition of appearing in print.

February 7, 2008

12

CHRONICLES OF FAYETTE

Julia Lee Sinks, *Chronicles of Fayette*.
La Grange: Fayette County Historical Commission, 1976.

IN 1975 I worked on a US Bicentennial project that was already nearly a century old. In 1876 a Centennial Committee of prominent citizens of Fayette County, Texas, asked Mrs. Julia Sinks, a prolific author and a charter member of the Texas State Historical Association who had come to Texas from Cincinnati in 1840, to compile a history of the county, based on her own reminiscences and those of other early settlers. Mrs. Sinks was an indefatigable interviewer and a fluent writer. She travelled all over Fayette County in a buggy, sitting in parlors and asking elderly ladies and gentlemen to describe things that had happened to them forty years before. She pressed James Ross so hard for details about his father's murder that he told her that "it was a subject that was disagreeable to him, and he seldom spoke of it." The contrast between the comfortable Victorian parlors of the 1870s and the hardscrabble lives that her subjects were telling her about must have been striking.

Mrs. Sinks completed her manuscript, but it was never published. Evidently the Citizens' Committee ran out of steam or funds or both, and the manuscript lay unnoticed in the Sinks papers at the University of Texas at Austin until a researcher looking for something else stumbled on it and called it to the attention of Walter Freytag, chair of the Fayette County Historical Commission. Freytag thought that publishing it would make a grand Bicentennial project, and he enlisted me to write the foreword. It was published in 1976 under the title *Chronicles of Fayette*.

The world described by Sinks and her interviewees was one of deprivation and constant danger from Indian attacks. Jesse Burnham, who established Burnham's ferry on the Colorado in 1824 and lived to be ninety-one, told Sinks that when he and his family first came to Texas they lived on deer meat, wild honey, and cornbread. They kept the honey in a deerskin, as they had no jars, jugs, or cans. They pulverized their cornmeal in a wooden mortar and sifted it through a sieve made by punching holes with a hot wire in a piece of deer hide stretched over a wooden hoop. His family wore clothing made from deerskin, as they had no cotton to weave into cloth. They once went for nine months without bread because they had no corn.

All of the settlers lived in constant fear of Indian attacks. The Comanches regularly raided the settlements, making off with horses and killing any white person who crossed their path. Sinks tells how Gonzalvo Woods was returning to the Colorado settlements from San Felipe with a small sack of coffee beans tied to his saddle. He was trotting along contemplating the aroma of fresh coffee filling his cabin when he realized that several Indians were trailing him. He spurred his horse to a canter and then a gallop, and every time a hoof hit the ground some coffee beans would spill out through a hole in the sack. The Indians got closer and closer and finally Woods cut the sack from his saddle. The Indians stopped to examine it, and Woods made it safely to his cabin. He traded his anticipated pot of coffee for his life.

The Indians who lived around the Colorado settlements were Tonkawas, who were ostensibly friendly to the settlers, but their presence in large numbers always made the colonists nervous. William Rabb, who was born in 1824, told Sinks how two hundred Tonkawas surrounded his family's house when he was an infant.

They were going on the war path against the Comanches, and they demanded a beef from Rabb's grandfather, which he gave them. They slaughtered it in the Rabbs' yard and feasted and danced all night. The Rabbs huddled in their cabin for twenty-four hours, afraid even to go to the spring for water. Only Rabb's grandfather, the head of the family, stood on the porch, holding an old sword and guarding the door. Rabb said that the Indians tried all night to get his grandfather to let them handle the sword, but he told them that he would kill the first one who touched it.

James Ross, the man whose son told Sinks that he did not want to talk about his father's murder, traded with the Tonkawas and permitted them to camp close to his house. This offended his neighbors, and they repeatedly warned him to cease his trading and send the Indians away. He refused, and eventually a group of armed settlers went to Ross's house to drive the Indians away. Sinks interviewed a man who had been a member of that party. He told her that when they approached Ross's house they found him marching back and forth on his porch, tapping the butt of his rifle on the floorboards and singing "Molly Put the Kettle On." They hailed him but he paid no attention, continuing to march and sing, and so they shot him down and left him dead on the porch. Sinks comments, "The best citizens of the county seemed to hold it a necessity; some whose lives bore no other act of violence held the act as a painful duty."

Estell Williams told Sinks about his grandfather, a Cumberland Presbyterian minister who did not hold with swearing. In the 1840s he lived on the main road between Houston and Austin and kept a hospitable house, but he had a board over his fireplace carved with the words, "Thou shalt not take the name of the Lord in vain in my house." One night a traveler reached his gate with a servant to whom he was using abusive language. The minister went out to the gate, and the traveler said that he wished to stay the night. "I cannot entertain you," the minister said.

"My name is Houston, sir, and I am tired and wish to stay," the traveller replied.

"I cannot keep you," the minister said. "I do not entertain men who use such language as I heard you use as you came up."

The traveler looked annoyed and said, "I am General Sam Houston, sir, and would you deny me a night's lodging?"

"I cannot help it, sir," was the reply. "My rules are too strong to break. So I bid you good evening."

Julia Lee Sinks was an oral historian before there were oral historians, and she had a keen ear for a story. It is a shame that her work had to steep for a hundred years before it was published, but it resulted in a very good book with a sound ring of authenticity.

February 13, 2014

✣ 13 ✣

THE TRAIL DRIVERS OF TEXAS

J. Marvin Hunter, *The Trail Drivers of Texas.*
Nashville: The Cokesbury Press, 1925

I RECENTLY made a trip to San Antonio to speak to the one hundredth anniversary meeting of the Old Trail Drivers Association of Texas, which was be held at the Witte Museum on November 12. The Old Trail Drivers Association is a unique Texas institution, the DAR of the cowboy world. When it was organized in February 1915 membership was limited to men who had driven cattle or horses up the trail from Texas between 1865 and 1896. The membership dues were one dollar per year. The next year the association, wisely recognizing that by restricting membership to an aging group it was condemning itself to extinction, voted to admit the sons of men who had been trail drivers between those dates. A few women were granted honorary membership. The first, in 1924, was Mrs. Lou Gore, who had operated a hotel in Abilene, Kansas, called the Drovers' Inn, a popular stopping place for Texas trail drivers. By 1980, when I became a member, most of the dwindling membership was composed of the grandchildren or great-grandchildren of the original members. I joined because I had inherited my great-uncle Gus Staples's handsome membership lapel button and I wanted to be able to wear it legitimately. Uncle Gus had been a charter member.

For many years the mainspring of the association was George W. Saunders of San Antonio, who was president of the George W. Saunders Livestock Commission Company and general manager of the Union Station Stockyards. Saunders, who was born in 1854 in Goliad County, had driven cattle to Kansas in the early 1870s. The association was organized in his San Antonio office in 1915, and he was the first vice president. He later served as president for several years. Most of the original members were men of his age. Membership in the association grew to 375 during its first year; by 1921 it had risen to more than one thousand. The members gathered once a year at the Gunter Hotel in San Antonio. The reunions provided them with a sense of community and family as well as a place to reminisce. G. O. Burrow, an active member for many years, wrote that in his old age "the only real enjoyment I have is our reunions of the Old Trail Drivers."

It was Saunders who, at the 1917 annual meeting, announced a plan to publish a book composed of the members' "reminiscences, incidents, and adventures of the Trail," which he said would be "not only highly interesting but valuable contributions to the frontier history of Texas." The book, entitled *The Trail Drivers of Texas,* was almost never published. The first editor quit in the middle of the project. The San Antonio firm hired to print the book went bankrupt, and the owner disappeared with all of the edited manuscript material. Saunders pushed on, however, and in April 1920 he hired newspaperman J. Marvin Hunter to take on the job of preparing the manuscripts for publication and finding a printer. Saunders gave Hunter three months in which to do the job.

While Saunders pressed the members for additional contributions, Hunter, routinely working late into the night, edited the material that Saunders brought him each day and took it to the Jackson Printing Company the next morning. Miraculously the book, in an edition of one thousand copies, was ready on July 21. Two years later Hunter produced a second volume of submissions that came in after the deadline, this time in an edition of five hundred copies, which he printed on his own linotype. In 1924 a revised and corrected edition of the first volume was published by the Globe Printing Company of San Antonio, and in 1925 Cokesbury Press of Nashville, Tennessee, combined both volumes into a one-volume, 1,044 page compilation of contributions from 360 old trail drivers. That 1925 edition has been reprinted several times, most recently by the University of Texas Press in 1985, with an introduction by B. Byron Price.

The Trail Drivers of Texas is a gold mine of information about the day-to-day details of cowboy life in the years after the Civil War. Going up the trail to Kansas with a herd of cattle was the greatest experience of most of the writers' lives, and they recorded their memories in vivid and pithy language, especially when describing the dangers of the trail. Here is Louis Schorp, a Texas-German cowboy from Rio Medina, describing his first stampede, when he was told to turn the leaders of the herd back into the herd, which would cause the confused cattle to mill around upon themselves: "As we were getting ready to start, the steers became frightened and stampeded. I was the only one on horseback and one of the men yelled at me to 'turn the leaders toward the bluff and mill them.' I did not understand the meaning of this for I had never seen a stampede before. I knew how to turn the crank of a coffee mill, but when it was necessary to mill a bunch of outlaw steers I did not know where to look for the crank."

And here is G. W. Mills of Lockhart describing a storm on the Kansas plains: "The storm hit us about 12 o'clock at night. There was some rain and to the northwest I noticed just a few little bats of lightning. Then it hit us full fury and we were in the midst of a wonderful electrical storm. We had the following varieties of lightning, all played close at hand, I tell you. It first commenced like flash lightning, then came forked lightning, then chain lightning, followed by the peculiar blue lightning. After that it rapidly developed into ball lightning, which rolled across the ground. After that spark lightning, then, most wonderful of all, it settled down on us like a fog. The air smelled of burning sulphur, you could see it on the horns of the cattle, the ears of our horses, and the brims of our hats. I grew some warm we thought we might burn up with it."

The Trail Drivers of Texas was the subject of my talk in San Antonio, and I hope that, by quoting passages like those above, I was able to give today's members, whose work is mostly in air-conditioned offices, a sense of what their ancestors' work days were like. I did pass on the advice offered by trail driver James Emmett McCauley, who wrote, "My advice to any young man or boy is to stay at home and not be a rambler as it won't buy you anything and above all stay away from a cow ranch, as not many cowpunchers ever save any money and 'tis a dangerous way to live."

November 13, 2015

✣ 14 ✣

WILLIAM SIDNEY PORTER, TEXAS WRITER

William Sydney Porter died in New York exactly a century ago last month, a victim of cirrhosis of the liver at the age of forty-seven. The death of an alcoholic writer in New York a hundred years ago would appear on the surface to have nothing to do with Texas but Porter, who became known to millions under his pen name, O. Henry, owed a great deal to our state. He came here at the age of twenty, worked on a ranch here, married here, and committed the crime that turned him into a writer here. He should be an honorary Texan.

Porter was born and grew up in Greensboro, North Carolina. His mother died from tuberculosis when he was three, and when he was in his late teens he developed a persistent cough. A family friend in Greensboro, James Hall, suggested that a change of climate might help and persuaded Porter to go to Texas to visit Hall's sons, Jesse Lee and Richard Hall, who lived on a ranch in the brush country south of San Antonio.

A young easterner could have no better introduction to Texas than knowing Lee Hall. By the time Porter met him, Hall had been in Texas for thirteen years and had become a legend as a member of Leander McNelly's special force of Texas Rangers in the Nueces Strip. Hall eventually became the company commander and broke up the Sutton-Taylor feud in DeWitt County. By the time Porter arrived, Hall had retired from the Rangers and was manager and part owner of the 250,000-acre Dull Ranch in La

Salle, Frio, and McMullen counties. Lee Hall and his friends were the model for the Texas Rangers that appeared in many of Porter's Texas stories, and many of the incidents in those stories are probably derived from tales that Hall told Porter.

After a two-year stay on the Dull Ranch Porter moved to Austin, where he remained for the next eleven years. When Lee Hall's brother Richard was elected Land Commissioner he gave Porter a job as a draftsman in the General Land Office. Porter was talented not only as a draftsman but as a sketch artist, and several of the county maps that he drew and embellished are still in the General Land Office files.

In Austin, Porter became the quintessential Gay Nineties man-about-town. A photograph shows him in a three-piece suit and a white bow tie, his hair in curls and his moustache curled and waxed, leaning on a cane and holding an opened Japanese paper umbrella in the other hand. He played the guitar and mandolin and joined a young men's musical group called the Hill City Quartette. In July 1887 he married seventeen-year-old Athol Estes, very much against her parents' wishes. They eloped and were married in the parlor of my cousin Jane Smoot's house on West Sixth Street by her grandfather, the Reverend Richmond K. Smoot. As a child I was reverently shown the corner of the room in which the ceremony took place. My cousin Jane's house is a monument to Austin's history, but that is another story.

When Richard Hall's term as land commissioner ended in 1891 Porter took a job as a teller at George W. Brackenridge's First National Bank of Austin, and that was his downfall. He disliked his job and left it after three years to establish his own humor magazine, *The Rolling Stone*, but when the bank was examined shortly after his departure it turned out to be short of funds, and Porter was indicted for embezzlement. He jumped bail, left his wife and young daughter behind, and fled to Honduras, but when he learned that his wife was dying from tuberculosis he came back to

Austin, gave himself up, and was sentenced to five years in the federal penitentiary. He was thirty-five years old.

In the penitentiary, Porter started writing the short stories that made him famous. He is remembered today as the chronicler of the people he called the Four Million, the clerks, shop girls, and grifters of New York, but his first subjects were the cowboys, ranchers, and politicians he had known in Texas. In a group of stories later gathered under the title *The Heart of the West* he drew heavily on his memories of the Dull Ranch and Austin.

These stories capture the atmosphere of Texas in the 1880s perfectly. Porter's characters are the frontiersmen who in middle age became ranchers and small-town bankers and public officials, respectable in their frock coats but still ready to draw a pistol to avenge a lady's honor. At least two of the stories are set in the General Land Office, and in one Porter explains in great detail the state's system of making land grants. Two others involve the unexpected arrival of a bank examiner at a small-town bank, a scene Porter must have lived over hundreds of times in prison. A dozen are set on South Texas ranches and include characters with names like Whispering Ben (a rancher known for his loud voice) and Dry Valley Johnson, so called to distinguish him from his neighbor Elm Creek Johnson.

Porter had a remarkable ear for ordinary speech. The dialogue in his New York stories is dated by his use of slang, but his ranch stories are studded with phrases that ring true today. A cowboy declares before wading into a fight that he will "go through this outfit like a cottontail through a brush corral." Another expresses his suspicions of a new hand by saying, "There's something mighty seldom about Piggy." A man berates himself for being "as big a fool as any Mormon." Good black river bottom land is "rich as cream."

Porter also had a bizarre sense of wordplay. In one of his stories he describes a meal supposedly listed on the menu of San Antonio's Menger Hotel as *dejeuner de poker*. "Each course was three of a kind, starting with guinea hen, guinea pig, and Guinness stout . . ."

Porter wrote some six hundred short stories and, in his day, was hailed as the equal of Rudyard Kipling and Guy de Maupassant. Today he is mostly forgotten. But in one of his Texas stories, "The Caballero's Way," he gave us an American icon, an outlaw called the Cisco Kid, who, transformed into a clever and glamorous caballero, has ridden the radio and television waves, the movie screens, and the comic book pages for nearly a century. Porter definitely deserves to be made an honorary Texan.

July 8, 2010

II.

A BOOKMAN'S PLEASURES

✣ 15 ✣

MY BOOKS AND MY FRIENDS

I THINK I HAVE Chronic Fatigue Syndrome. I only read about it yesterday but I'm sure I've got it. Laura Hillenbrand, the author of *Seabiscuit,* is afflicted with it. She cannot leave her Washington, DC, apartment and does all of her research on the Internet or by telephone. Right now I feel like I could not leave my house in Fort Davis or even pick up a telephone. I have just spent four days reshelving all of the books in my study, about three thousand volumes, and I am bone-tired.

Several weeks ago we had some bookshelves installed in our garage, and I decided to try to relieve some of the clutter in my study by moving my books on architecture and museums onto them, which would enable me to devote the shelves in the study entirely to Texas and American history and to get the stacks of books on those subjects that have accumulated over the past few years off of the floor and onto the shelves. I shelve my books alphabetically by author, so this meant moving every book in the study.

I should emphasize that I am not a collector. I do not try to acquire every edition of a book, nor do I pay much attention to condition, as long as the book will not come apart in my hands while I am reading it. My library is a working reference library, and it is essential that I be able to find the book that I need in it when I want it. My shelves had become so jammed that I was beginning to order second copies of books that I knew I owned but could not lay my hands on. I found a dozen duplicate copies this week, usually shelved behind other books.

Reshelving takes a great deal of time because I have to stop every now and then and think about the web of friendships that certain books call up. For instance, while sorting through the *Hs* I came across a small book bound in red cloth with the title stamped on the spine, *A Trip to Texas*, published by Macdonald in London in 1962. My name is written on the front endpaper with the words, "Austin, 1965" under it, reminding me that I bought the book at the Brick Row Book Shop in Austin, a shop in an old house on Rio Grande Street owned by my friend Franklin Gilliam, who is worth a column in himself. The book is an account of a visit to the University of Texas in 1960 by the British poet and scholar of Victorian poetry Kenneth Hopkins. It includes photographs of Gilliam and several other Austin friends from the sixties, as well as a caricature of the author by the late Bob Eckhardt, who was once my next-door neighbor in Austin and remains my hero in Texas politics.

I am pretty sure that the book was recommended to me by Robert Wells, an Englishman who worked for Gilliam and who later married Dianne Rivers, an Austin lady who kept a pet boa constrictor named Snake in her apartment and who is the sister of Claudia Rivers, the special collections librarian at the University of Texas at El Paso. I have kept up with the Wellses over the years and have on my shelves a manuscript autobiography by Robert, who in 1946 was the youngest officer in the Indian army, serving with the Thirteenth Frontier Force Rifles in Kashmir. I see Claudia Rivers whenever I go to El Paso to do research. All of these people, encompassed by one book.

Although most of my Texas books are shelved alphabetically by author, I decided to shelve all of the volumes about Sam Houston together with the *Hs* because I can never remember the names of some of their authors. One whose name I will not forget is Amelia Williams, who gave me a signed copy of her *Following Sam Houston* when I was seven years old. She was a cousin of my grandmother and was one of the first women to get a PhD in history from the University of Texas. She was the coeditor of the Sam Houston papers, wrote her dissertation on the siege of the Alamo, and compiled the list of defenders that appears on the cenotaph in Alamo Plaza. I remember her as an old lady with her white hair in braids, and I see her every time I pick her book up.

Then there are the six volumes I reshelved that relate to Al Lowman. Lowman is a very old friend and is the quintessential book collector, the kind of collector who does want every edition of a particular book. His best-known book is *Printing Arts in Texas*, originally published in Austin in 1975 and reprinted in 1981. I have the 1981 edition, and I also have *Fruits of a Gentle Madness*, the catalogue put out by the Cushing Memorial Library at Texas A&M after Lowman placed his fine printing collection there in 2004. The catalogue includes a delightful essay by Lowman called "Putting Your Friends on the Shelf," about his friendships with authors and printers. Lowman was responsible for the most beautiful book in my library, *This Bitterly Beautiful Land: A Texas Commonplace Book*, published in 1972. This is an oversized book printed by letterpress on handmade paper in an edition of 275 copies. Each page contains a quotation about Texas selected by Lowman, illustrated with a woodcut by Barbara Whitehead, who is also a very old friend and who designed and illustrated my own recent book, *Texas, My Texas*. Lowman's book was printed by Bill Holman, another friend. Three more volumes complete my Lowman collection: a reminiscence of the bookseller Dudley Dobie, entitled *Remembering Dudley Dobie, the First Bookseller to Enrich My Life and Empty My Pockets*, given to me by the lovely Velvet Glass of Alpine; the catalogue of an auction of Lowman's collection of Texas illustrators, with occasional tart comments by Lowman; and a copy of the *Southwestern Historical Quarterly* containing Lowman's presidential address to the 2003 annual meeting of the Texas State Historical Association, a hilarious series of anecdotes about a West Texas cowboy called Bell Cord Rutherford. Lowman was a consummate raconteur, and his talks were full of erudition laced with wit. Sadly, he now suffers from a degenerative disease that has affected his speech, and I can enjoy his humor only in print.

As Lowman put it, my bookshelves are full of friends, and that is why it has taken me so long to sort through my books.

May 24, 2012

16

AL LOWMAN, TEXAS BOOKMAN

I RECENTLY bought a book that belonged to Al Lowman. To be precise, I bought two books, because my purchase was the two-volume set by Harry Oberholser entitled *The Bird Life of Texas,* published by the University of Texas Press in 1974. I paid $110 for it and it was a steal, because if you can find it at an antiquarian bookseller's it will be priced at twice that if not more. I got it at the book auction held by the Texas State Historical Association at their annual meeting in Dallas earlier this month. I bid on it for two reasons. I have always wanted a copy, even though I am not a birder, because it is a landmark in Texas publishing. But even more than that, I wanted to own a book that had belonged to Al Lowman.

Lowman, who lives in San Marcos (although he usually sports a name tag at meetings that says "Al Lowman, Stringtown") is Texas's most distinguished bibliophile, and its most generous. He recently donated his collection of ten thousand books on Texas and the Southwest to the Texas State Historical Association, to be sold at auction to benefit the association. The auction at which I bought the Oberholser volumes was only one of a series; others have been conducted in New York by Swann Galleries, and more of his books will be auctioned at TSHA meetings over the next three years. In 2006 Lowman donated his collection of Texas illustrators, including works by artists Tom Lea, José Cisneros, Harold Bugbee, and Buck Schewitz, to a fund-raising auction held by the

TSHA. A few years earlier he presented his collection of fine press books to the Texas A&M Library.

I first met Lowman in 1968, when I was working for the Texas State Historical Association in Austin. At that time the association had its offices on the University of Texas campus in rooms that it had occupied since 1911. I worked at a rolltop desk that had been in the same place since 1911, in a room that was lined with shelves containing unsold copies of the association's publications, some of which had been printed several years before 1911. I came back from lunch one day to find a tall, sandy-haired fellow standing on my desk in his stocking feet, taking down volumes of a 1947 association publication called *El Sal del Rey* one by one from the highest shelf, opening each one and then closing it and replacing it on the shelf. "Can I help you find something?" I asked him. "I'm looking for a copy with the misprint on Page 54," he replied, and he worked his way to the end of the shelf before climbing down and introducing himself as Al Lowman.

We subsequently became good friends, and I learned to appreciate Lowman's dry humor and his seemingly infinite store of knowledge about Southwestern books and their authors. At the height of his collecting days he was an indefatigable pursuer of author's inscriptions and signatures, and he was very particular about how and where his books were signed. He once yanked a ballpoint pen out of my hand when I started to use it to inscribe one of my books to him. He handed me a fountain pen, instructing me to write on what he called the "bastard half-title" page, that is, the largely blank sheet in front of the title page. "That's what they put it in there for," he said. We once had a temporary falling-out over my failure to secure signatures for him from half a dozen Dallas authors whose books he mailed to me after I moved to Dallas. I could not bring myself to approach these formidable strangers, and Lowman thought it was a perfectly reasonable and legitimate request. He once charged into ex-President Lyndon

AL LOWMAN

Johnson's Austin office to secure Johnson's signature on a portrait sketch by José Cisneros, and he got it.

Something of the flavor of a conversation with Lowman about books, authors, and illustrators can be obtained from reading the catalogue for the 2006 auction of his Texas illustrators collection, to which he contributed occasional annotations. He comments on the exhaustive length of the inscriptions that Senator Ralph Yarborough wrote in books that he presented to friends, saying that the senator obviously felt that brevity was no virtue in book inscriptions. He reveals that when he wrote the catalogue for an exhibit of printer Carl Hertzog's work at the Institute of Texan Cultures in 1972, the director of the institute refused to pay for a José Cisneros portrait of Hertzog that Lowman had commissioned as a frontispiece, calling it a "frill." Lowman paid for it out of his own pocket and then had twenty prints of it made, which he sold for enough to reimburse himself. In an entry on a biography of Texas primitive artist H. O. Kelly, he tells us that when a portrait of Kelly by a Brownwood artist was unveiled in a ceremony at Howard Payne University, Kelly's wife was heard to remark to her daughter, "It looks so much like the old son of a bitch I wouldn't have it in the house." That is pure Lowman.

Lowman is not only a collector, he is an erudite author with a detailed knowledge of the printer's craft, and his *Printing Arts in Texas*, published in 1972, is the standard reference work about fine printing and small presses in Texas.

He is also partially responsible for the most beautiful book ever published in Texas, *This Bitterly Beautiful Land*, a collection of quotations from books and at least one poem about Texas. Lowman selected and edited the quotations, which were then hand-set in type by Austin book designer Bill Holman and printed on English handmade paper, one quotation per page. Each page is illustrated with a woodcut by Austin artist Barbara Whitehead.

Holman printed 275 copies of the book on a hand press, a back-breaking task, and sold them for $55 apiece. I am proud to own one, and I think of the richness of Al Lowman's knowledge every time I open it.

March 25, 2010

Al Lowman died at his home in San Marcos on April 16, 2013. He was seventy-eight years old.

✣ 17 ✣

BROWSING IN USED BOOKSTORES

ONE OF THE great pleasures in my life has been browsing in used bookstores. This has been true ever since I was a small boy. My father was a dedicated bookstore hound—he collected Civil War memoirs—and he started taking me with him on his Saturday book prowls when I was five years old. I am still hooked on the habit.

The first used bookstore that I can remember was Lowdermilk's in Washington, DC. This was in an old town house on F Street near Fourteenth. It had been a used bookstore for sixty years when I first entered it with my father in 1945. There were three floors and a basement full of sturdy wooden bookshelves. The founder, W. H. Lowdermilk, had collected books on the Civil War, and much of his original stock was still there, which delighted my father. At my age I was more interested in the bins of colored prints, mostly birds, animals, and battles. I still have a small print of a pair of Green Jamaican Todies that I bought there, my first bookstore purchase. I visited Lowdermilk's regularly until it closed for good in 1969 and always found something there I needed. Johnny Jenkins of Austin bought most of its stock, including unopened cartons of Government Printing Office publications going back to the 1870s that were found in the basement.

Texas has had some memorable used bookstores. Barber's in Fort Worth occupied what had once been the lobby and mezzanine of an old hotel building on the corner of Eighth and Throckmorton from 1925 until it closed about 2000. I was once astonished to find there, some time in the 1960s, a leather-bound set of Guy de Maupassant's fiction with my great-aunt Emily Keene's bookplate in each volume. Aunt Emily died in Denver in 1924, and the books must have passed to her sister, my grandmother, who died in Fort Worth in 1950. They somehow ended up at Barber's.

Shortly before Barber's closed I bought a copy of J. Frank Norfleet's *Norfleet* there and remarked to Bryan Perkins, the owner, that I thought that the book had been on his shelves since I was in high school. Perkins flipped open the cover and said, "Yep. I bought this book in 1955." He then showed me the marks in pencil on the inside cover that he used to encode the date that he bought a book and the price he had paid for it. When my father died in 1993 I called Perkins to come to the house and buy all of Dad's Civil War books that I did not want to keep, and so some of his Lowdermilk purchases were recycled back into the world of used bookstores.

No account of Texas bookstores would be complete without a mention of Brock's in San Antonio. Brock's was on Commerce Street about a block from Schilo's Restaurant, two stories and a basement full of used books. Norman Brock was a big, shambling man whom no one could describe as a bibliophile as he abused books, stacking them everywhere, sometimes on their ends. What was on his shelves was just the tip of the iceberg, but most of the rest of the ice was totally inaccessible unless you crawled around on your hands and knees. Brock never marked prices in any of his books. You had to take the book to him and he would examine both it and you, trying to figure out how badly you wanted it and how much you might pay for it, and then mark a price in it. This meant that you had to take the book you wanted to the counter with two or three other books that you didn't want and keep a poker face while he priced all of them, hoping that he would not guess which one it was that interested you. This was not hard to do as Brock, for a book dealer, was sadly ignorant about books. I once found a copy of Albion Tourgee's *The Invisible Empire,* an account of the Ku Klux Klan published in 1880, there. I sandwiched it between two other books and took it to Brock to price. He glanced at the title, said, "Science fiction, huh?" and marked it at fifty cents. It is one of the few book bargains I have ever gotten. Brock's closed sometime in the 1970s, literally under the weight of its own stock. The fire department ruled the building unsafe because the weight of the books on the second floor had weakened the structure.

The Brick Row Book Shop in Austin was the complete opposite of Brock's. It was in a frame house on Rio Grande Street, just a few blocks from the University of Texas's Humanities Research Center, which was its principal customer. The owner, Franklin Gilliam, lived on the premises and during the morning hours could be found padding around the aisles between the shelves in a dressing gown and slippers, a cup of coffee in one hand. He was usually dressed by noon. Gilliam had bought the Brick Row in 1954 and moved it from New Haven, Connecticut, to Austin, where the University of Texas was spending millions of dollars a year on the Brick Row's specialty, English and American literature. Gilliam, a native of Cuero, Texas, was an experienced antiquarian book dealer with exquisite taste. According to my friend Robert Wells, whom I first met when he worked at the Brick Row, Gilliam once opened a carton of new books that the shop had been obliged to take in a complicated trade, picked up a volume with a particularly gaudy jacket, dropped it back in the box, and said, "I'd rather deal in fertilizer." Sadly, Gilliam moved the shop to San Francisco in 1971.

By the time I discovered the Brick Row, I had graduated from browsing bookshops to ordering books from dealers' catalogues. Gilliam gave me an invaluable piece of advice about catalogues.

Dealers frequently employ the term, "Not in ______," citing the author of a well-known bibliography of a particular subject, in an entry to indicate the rarity and justify the price of the offering. "When you see that in a catalogue," Gilliam said, "you should always ask yourself, 'should the book be in that bibliography, or is it about some other subject entirely?'" Over the years, Gilliam's words have saved me a lot of money.

January 23, 2004

✣ 18 ✣

ROSENGREN'S BOOKS, SAN ANTONIO

I DISCOVERED Rosengren's Books when I moved to San Antonio in 1966 because it was on the first floor of the hotel I was living in. The Crockett Hotel, directly behind the Alamo, had two memorable features. One was a parking lot with a sign by the attendant's booth that said "Davy Crockett Tied His Horse Here When He Fought for Us at the Alamo," and the other was Rosengren's Books.

During my first week at the Crockett I learned that Rosengren's was far more than a bookstore. It was the intellectual center of San Antonio and South Texas, and its customers included the brightest and most interesting people in town. It was presided over by Florence Rosengren, a widow in her sixties with a gentle manner and a beautiful smile. Florence had a remarkable ability to match books with people. Every time I went in the store, she would say, "Something just came in that I think you would like," and hand me a book. Florence introduced me to Marshall McLuhan, Thomas Pynchon, Kurt Vonnegut, Ken Kesey, and Gabriel Garcia Marquez. When I got a job as a curator of a furniture museum she assembled a basic library on American furniture for me, and when I moved to the country to take the job she selected a shelf of books for me to read on long winter nights. They included *War and Peace,* Montesquieu's *Essays,* and Robert Burton's *Anatomy of Melancholy*. I read *War and Peace* and Montesquieu with pleasure, but I still have to tackle Burton.

I patronized Rosengren's until it closed its doors for good in 1987. I thought I knew a lot about the store and about the Rosengren family, because Florence's son, Figgi, and his wife, Cam, who took over the active management of the store in 1979, became close friends, and Cam, now a widow, is our host whenever Dedie and I visit San Antonio.

But when I picked up Mary Carolyn Hollers George's recently published *Rosengren's Books* (San Antonio: Wings Press, 2014), I realized how much I did not know about Rosengren's that was worth knowing. I knew that the store had started in Chicago and moved to San Antonio in 1935, but I did not know that the founder, Frank Rosengren, Florence's husband, was a rare book specialist who opened his first book store in the early 1920s, when rare book prices were on their way to an all-time high, nor did I know that he worked all of his life on an uncompleted book about American first editions. George tells a story about him that I had heard versions of over the years, but she pins down the facts. One day in 1929 Rosengren was rummaging around in the basement of his Chicago shop and he came across a bound volume of old pamphlets, which he had priced at twenty dollars. He casually thumbed through it and realized that one of the pamphlets was actually a thirty-nine-page first edition of two stories by Edgar Allen Poe, *The Murders in the Rue Morgue* and *The Man Who Was Used Up*, published by Poe himself in 1843, one of the rarest of American imprints. There were only three known copies, and he was holding the fourth one in his hands. He sold it to J. K. Lilly, the pharmaceuticals millionaire, for $13,000. A few days later the stock market crashed and the bottom fell out of the rare book market. Rosengren took his recent bride, Florence, on a delayed six-week honeymoon in Europe and came back with enough money to float the shop through the next three years of the Depression.

FLORENCE ROSENGREN

I knew that the move to San Antonio had been prompted by the health of Rosengren's son, Figgi, but I did not know that it had been engineered by San Antonio lawyer and book collector Harry Herzberg, whose collection of circus material is now at the Witte Museum. Herzberg started urging Rosengren to move to San Antonio in 1929, writing him teasingly that in comparison to Chicago "the people are more courteous, the highways better, the climate more salubrious, the odor of the stockyards missing . . . I am not surprised that you do not know that there are no Indians here." When the Rosengrens finally made the move, it was Herzberg who found them space for the shop in the Milam Building, where his office was located, and who found them a house, the eighteenth-century Zambrano House in the River Road neighborhood.

I knew that the Zambrano House has been the scene of literary parties for decades (they are now orchestrated by Cam Rosengren), but I did not know how they got started. George explains that during World War II the shop became a haven for book-minded servicemen who were stationed at the numerous military bases in San Antonio. They would gather there on Saturday mornings when they had weekend passes. At that time all businesses in downtown San Antonio closed on Saturday afternoons, and Florence got into the habit of inviting whoever was in the shop when she closed to the Rosengren house to spend the rest of the afternoon and have Saturday night supper. The talk was so good that guests inevitably stayed over for Sunday dinner, sleeping in a barn that had been converted into a studio, and the Zambrano House became the site of a four-year-long series of weekend parties. Guests contributed rationed groceries from post commissaries, and all distinctions of rank were ignored: privates argued about poetry and plays with majors and colonels.

George, who is a native San Antonian and has written biographies of San Antonio architects Alfred Giles and O'Neal Ford, has acquired a great deal of information about San Antonio's artistic and Bohemian community in the mid-twentieth century, and she has packed it into this beautifully designed book.

February 5, 2018

✣ 19 ✣

BROWSING IN LIBRARIES

I AM A COMPULSIVE reader. I take a book along whenever I think I am going to have to wait anywhere, such as doctors' offices or restaurants when I am dining alone. When I have to wait unexpectedly, I will search desperately for something to read. The other day I found myself avidly perusing a 1994 issue of *Astronomy Magazine* while waiting for a prescription to be filled in an Alpine drug store. If that had not been available I would probably have been reading the labels on the Tylenol bottles. I am usually reading at least two books at the same time at home; a serious non-fiction book in the afternoon and a novel or detective story in the evening.

By "book" I mean one of those old-fashioned devices that consists of printed pages bound between two covers. You have to turn the pages by hand. I tried a Kindle not long ago and didn't like it. I kept thinking that the text was going to disappear from the screen before I got to the end of it. Some people think that books are going to disappear, to be replaced by electronic texts, but I doubt it, even though the techies keep saying that books have already gone the way of manuscript scrolls and the rest of us just don't know it. There is too much pleasure in handling a book, and it is a pleasure that each generation discovers anew.

I honestly cannot remember learning to read. My parents always had books in the house, and when I was about two my mother started reading to me from the standard children's books of the day, *Ping* and *Make Way for Ducklings* and *Many Moons*, pointing to each word as she went along. One day I picked a book up and discovered I could read it by myself, and I have seldom been without one since.

As a child, no one told me that there was anything I could not read, and I never made a distinction between children's books and so-called adult books. I started the third grade late and on my first day discovered that everyone was supposed to give a book report at the end of the week on something they had checked out from the school library the week before. I gave a report on *The Adventures of General Marbot*, the memoir of a Napoleonic general that was in my father's library and that I had been reading at home. The teacher insisted that I bring a note from my mother saying that I had actually read it.

Some of my early reading was a little retrograde. When I was seven one of my father's boyhood friends in Fort Worth gave me a trunk of children's books that he had enjoyed when he was my age, which was in 1912 or thereabouts. I lapped up about thirty volumes of *The Rover Boys* ("Rover by name and rover by nature, sir!"), *The Airplane Boys*, *The Moving Picture Boys*, and *Tom Swift*. A few years later I discovered *The Hardy Boys* and got back into step with my own contemporaries.

I got the habit of going to libraries at an early age, because I ran out of books at home. I was a solitary little boy and not very good at games, and some of my most pleasant childhood memories are of libraries. I can still remember the thrill of discovering William Pene du Bois's *The Twenty-One Balloons*, which I think is the finest children's book ever written, in the Shirlington branch of the Arlington County, Virginia, public library when I was nine. I could take you to the exact spot on the shelf where it was today if that library was still there. I checked it out about six times. In Fort Worth, in high school, I became a habitué of the downtown

Fort Worth Public Library, taking the bus there after school. There was a special Fort Worth-Tarrant County history room, from which the books could not be checked out, and I spent most winter afternoons of my senior year there reading about my hometown. I will always associate the history of Fort Worth with the smell of wet wool coats laid on top of steam radiators.

There was a typescript history of Fort Worth on the shelves of that room, bound in several volumes. It had been prepared in the 1930s by the WPA's Federal Writer's Project, and it contained information about certain deceased prominent Fort Worth citizens that was not discussed in public, such as Winfield Scott's ownership of saloons and bawdy houses in Hell's Half Acre (Mrs. Winfield Scott's name was on the cornerstone of the library) and Burk Burnett's shooting a man in the back in the washroom of the Goodwin Hotel in Paducah, Texas, in 1912. It was there that I learned that you could find out things in a library that you could not learn anyplace else.

It was also there that I learned the pleasures of browsing the shelves of an open-stack library, where books are shelved side-by-side according to subject matter, and you discover four books that you did not know about while looking for the one that you want. Most large libraries operate on the closed-stack system, where you have to find the book that you want in the card catalogue, fill out a call slip, and wait for the book to be brought to you. Years later I had a job at the Library of Congress, a closed-stack library, that entitled me to a stack pass, and I was in hog heaven roaming the shelves. I found books on subjects that I never knew existed and would never have found in the card catalogue, much less the new computerized catalogue.

All of this is why I was so depressed to read a news release the other day about a Massachusetts prep school that has completely done away with its twenty-thousand-volume library and replaced it with a half-million-dollar "learning center" equipped with computers, giant TV screens, electronic readers, and a coffee shop. The headmaster says that they are "shaping emerging trends and optimizing technology," whatever that means. I say that they are committing cultural vandalism, and if I had children there I would yank them out so fast that they wouldn't have time to dance.

September 16, 2010

✣ 20 ✣

SOME RARE TEXAS BOOKS NOT IN MY LIBRARY

I CANNOT DESCRIBE myself as a book collector, even though I have a large library of books about Texas. I am an accumulator, and (as I've mentioned before) I care little about the condition of a book as long as it will not come apart in my hands while I am reading it. A real bibliophile would turn up his nose at my library.

One moderately rare book that I do own is Charles Nagel's *A Boy's Civil War Story*, privately published in St. Louis in 1934, which I bought in a London bookshop for the equivalent of about two dollars in the early 1970s (one of the rules about collecting books on Texas is to buy them as far away from Texas as possible). It is a memoir of Nagel's boyhood in the Texas-German community of Millheim, in Austin County, and of the hair-raising trip he made across Texas to Monterrey, Mexico, with his father when he was thirteen so that his father, a Union sympathizer, could escape conscription into the Confederate army. Very few copies were published, and even fewer have survived.

Following the rule of buying books about Texas as far away from Texas as possible, I once walked into a bookshop across the street from the British Museum in London and asked if they had anything about Texas. The clerk checked the computer and came up with a copy of Archibald Clavering Gunter's novel *Mr. Potter of Texas* in the 1888 London edition, which I bought for ten pounds. It is not exactly a rare book (the University of Texas Library has a dozen copies), but it does have an interesting Texas connection.

The hero is a blustery, loud-talking Texan who is visiting England. Gunter based him on Texas rancher Shanghai Pierce, and Pierce was reading the novel when he died.

Some books are more interesting for the circumstances under which they were written than for their content. A good example is Mamie Yeary's *Reminiscences of the Boys in Gray, 1861-1865*, published in 1912 by the Smith and Lamar Publishing House of the Methodist Episcopal Church, South, in Dallas. It is a compilation of approximately 2,500 short biographies of Confederate veterans living in Texas, written by themselves. Yeary is identified on the title page as "Miss Mamie Yeary of McGregor, Texas, member of Pearl West Chapter No. 569, United Daughters of the Confederacy." Her brief biography in the *New Handbook of Texas* says that she was an invalid and lived with her parents into adulthood. She must have passed her days by writing to every Confederate veteran in Texas, asking for his recollections of the war, and then editing them for publication.

The rarest of all Texas books is William W. Heartsill's *Fourteen Hundred and 91 Days in the Confederate Army,* published in Marshall, Texas, in 1876 in an edition of one hundred copies. I do not own a copy of it, but I was once allowed to look at one. Heartsill was twenty-two when he enlisted in the Confederate army in Marshall in 1861. He kept a daily journal in a series of notebooks all through the war, mailing each notebook home when it was full. After the war he came back to Marshall and opened a saddle and harness shop. Sometime in the early 1870s he decided to edit his diaries and publish them.

He got hold of something called an Octavo Novelty Press, a hand-operated printing press that was essentially a child's toy. It would print one page of handset type at a time. He started printing his book on December 9, 1874, and completed it eighteen months later on June 28, 1876. He wrote in the preface that "the work was done in spare moments, during business engagements; printers will know the attending difficulties. . . . In cold weather the ink was too thick, in the summer I would sometimes get too much on the roller. . . ." Heartsill had to print one hundred copies of each page and then tear down the type and set up the next page, all between waiting on customers. The book is 265 pages long.

Heartsill wrote to his surviving comrades asking them to send photographs of themselves for illustrations. Sixty-one men replied, including Captain Sam Richardson, who sent a photograph of himself wearing spotted jaguar-hide britches with silver buttons down the sides and armed with two pistols in jaguar-hide holsters, a Bowie knife, and a rifle. Heartsill had one hundred copies made of each photograph and pasted them on blank pages interleaved with the text. Not more than fifteen copies of *Fourteen Hundred and 91 Days in the Confederate Army* have survived; twelve are in libraries. The last copy that was sold at auction, in 2005, went for $30,000.

Not long ago my friend Judith Ross of Marfa brought me word of a Texas book that may be even rarer than Heartsill's. She had been visiting in South Africa, and had clipped an item out of a Johannesburg newspaper about a local book dealer named Ian Snelling who had found a copy of the 1937 edition of Robert E. Howard's novel, *A Gent From Bear Creek*, in a charity bookshop. Snelling thought that Robert E. Howard might be a pseudonym for Louis L'Amour, so he bought the book for a few cents and took it home to research it. He learned that Robert E. Howard was a pulp-fiction writer who lived in Cross Plains, Texas, in the 1930s and is the focus of an enthusiastic cult of admirers because he invented the character Conan the Barbarian. *A Gent From Bear Creek* was his first and only novel, published in England and never sold in the United States. Howard never saw it because he committed suicide before it was released. Because so many books were pulped in England during the war to meet the paper shortage there were only six known copies; Snelling had found the seventh. He sold it for considerably more than he paid for it to a Howard fan who donated it to the Robert E. Howard Museum in Cross Plains. Because Howard's works appeal to a far narrower readership than books about the Civil War, it did not bring what copies of Heartsill would, but it was up there.

September 16, 2010

✣ 21 ✣

MY LIFE IN COOKBOOKS

I COULD WRITE my life in terms of cookbooks I have owned. When I first left Texas to live by myself in New York, my mother gave me a small blue loose-leaf notebook in which she had written the recipes for my favorite dishes. It was my first cookbook. She also gave me a piece of paper on which she had written the instructions for ironing a shirt ("Iron cuffs and collar first. . . ."). I am afraid I gave the ironing instructions more attention than the cookbook because I quickly discovered the exotic delights of the Jewish delicatessens and Italian restaurants that dotted my New York neighborhood, and I settled into a pretty steady diet of split pea soup, hot pastrami sandwiches, and spaghetti carbonara, with an occasional trip to Harout Deradian's Armenian Cafeteria for their eighty-five-cent lamb and rice special when I wanted variety. My mother's roast chicken, black-eyed peas, cornbread, and baked ham went uncooked. I was not into entertaining at home in those days.

By the time I was in my mid-twenties, however, I had learned that "Won't you come to dinner at my place?" was a much better line than "Let me show you my etchings," and I decided I had better learn to cook. I bought two cookbooks, which I still have. One, because I liked spaghetti and thought it would be easy to prepare, was Edwin and Mildred Knopf's *The Food of Italy and How to Prepare It*, published by Edwin Knopf's brother Arnold A. Knopf in 1964. The other was Century Downing's *The Conspirators'*

Cookbook, published by Knopf in 1967. The latter is one of the oddest cookbooks I have ever seen. It is a curmudgeonly critique of American cooking (one of the chapters is "The American Tragedy of Bread"). The title, the author explains, comes from the necessity to form a culinary conspiracy to change American eating habits. The book is more about methods of cooking than about recipes. From it I learned how to poach eggs, how to boil shelled shrimp, and how to cook rice. Some pages are deeply stained with the efforts of my first dinner parties. The recipes for Hungarian chicken paprika and lasagna al forno ferragamo are almost unreadable.

I have always suspected that Century Downing was a pseudonym for Edwin Knopf. There is a certain similarity of tone in both books, an anecdotal approach to cooking that involves discreet name-dropping. Lasagna al forno ferragamo, for instance, is a recipe obtained from Salvatore Ferragamo, maker of expensive shoes. On the other hand, I suppose someone could actually be named Century Downing. Whoever he was, he got me through my first experimental dinner parties, and I am grateful to him.

At one point in my life I ate a lot of lunches at The Hedges in Neiman-Marcus's Fort Worth store, and I discovered Helen Corbitt, the New Yorker who ran Neiman's restaurants. I bought Corbitt's 1957 cookbook, *Helen Corbitt's Cookbook,* to get the recipe for the poppy-seed dressing that was served on the fruit salad at The Hedges, but I discovered that it included the recipe for a Texas classic that Corbitt invented, pickled black-eyed peas. Corbitt did not like the taste of black-eyed peas, so she developed a method of pickling them in vinegar. They are now marketed as Texas caviar. Corbitt's cookbook expanded my cooking horizons immensely, and those of thousands of other Texans. There should be a statue of her somewhere, perhaps in front of Neiman's downtown Dallas store.

I discovered Julia Child after I moved to San Antonio. A lady I entertained occasionally gave me Childs's *French Chef Cookbook* (a hint, perhaps?). I concentrated on the thirty-minute dinner section, and I became adept at all of them except the swordfish dinner. I have never liked swordfish. I then married and graduated to Childs's two-volume *Mastering the Art of French Cooking*. I have a vivid memory of my then wife and me trying to make the brioche in the second volume in the kitchen of a South Texas ranch house on a sweltering July day. We were kneading the butter into the dough and the dough was not doing what it was supposed to do when we realized that Julia Child worked in the cool stone-floored kitchen of a Norman farmhouse and we were working in one where the temperature was in the high nineties. We put the dough tray on a wheeled cart and pushed it into a bedroom where we could continue the operation directly under a window air-conditioning unit.

Shortly after that I found myself single again and living in Dallas, where my friend Conover Hunt, who was once Sweetheart of Sigma Chi at the University of Virginia, gave me a copy of *Virginia Hospitality*, published by the Junior League of Hunt's home town of Hampton, Virginia. It is one of the best cookbooks I have ever owned. Hampton is a place no one ever leaves, so there are two hundred years' worth of family recipes in it, including a chicken dish called Country Captain that involves curry, bell peppers, and almonds and quickly became one of my favorites. There are also at least two dozen recipes for crabs and oysters, reflecting Hampton's location on Chesapeake Bay.

I eventually moved to Washington, DC, and married again, this time to a woman who is a superb cook. She brought a library of cookbooks to our marriage, and I pretty much retired from the kitchen. I cannot say that we collect cookbooks, at least not on the scale of an Austin friend who has five thousand of them—he has one apartment to live in and another one down the hall to keep his cookbooks in—but we have seven shelves of them and occasionally add a new one. After retiring and moving to Fort Davis we acquired *Culinary Delights: Feeding the Flock*, published in 2001 by the Fort Davis United Methodist Women. We especially like the section called "Cooking for a Crowd," composed of recipes, most of which were supplied by Betty Prude of the Prude Ranch, that begin with ingredients like "48 pounds ham" and are designed to feed two hundred people. That's real Texas cooking.

October 27, 2011

III.

BACK ROADS AND DARK CORNERS

22

MY FIRST THIRTY YEARS

Gertrude Beasley, *My First Thirty Years.*
Paris: Contact Press, 1925.

I FIRST HEARD about Gertrude Beasley's book, *My First Thirty Years,* from my late friend Al Lowman, who had heard about it from the bookseller and one-time Sul Ross librarian Dudley Dobie, who had heard about it from his cousin J. Frank Dobie. The book was published by Robert McAlmon's Contact Press in 1925, and it probably never sold more than one hundred copies. It is one of the rarest of all Texas books.

It is a Texas book because Gertrude Beasley was a Texan and, for at least part of her first thirty years, an Abilene schoolteacher. She was born in 1893 on a cotton farm near Coleman, one of thirteen children, and grew up in poverty. Her mother eventually divorced Beasley's abusive and shiftless father and moved to Abilene, where Beasley enrolled in Simmons College (now Hardin Simmons University). She received a BA and a teacher's certificate in 1914, having taught in country schools during alternate semesters while she was in college. Three-fourths of the 321-page text is devoted to this remarkable young woman's life on a series of cotton farms and in Abilene. When she was twenty-one she moved to Chicago to enroll in a master's degree program at the University of Chicago, and from there she moved to Bellingham, Washington, to teach in the State Normal School there. Her narrative ends in June 1920, with her boarding a ship for Japan. She

SC
E·G·BEASLEY

evidently travelled in China and Russia writing for *National Geographic* before ending up in Paris in 1925, where she published her memoir.

Robert McAlmon, her publisher, was an expatriate American whose short-lived Contact Press published avant-garde works by Ernest Hemingway, William Carlos Williams, Ford Madox Ford, Djuna Barnes, and Gertrude Stein. In his memoir, *Being Geniuses Together,* McAlmon wrote that only two of his authors ever got temperamental with him "and they were both Gertrudes, Stein and Beasley . . . both megalomaniacs with an idea that to know them was to serve them without question in their demands."

I have seen and handled a copy of McAlmon's 1925 edition of Beasley's book. It is in the Archives of the Big Bend at Sul Ross State University, purchased, I am sure, by Dudley Dobie when he was the librarian there in the 1950s. It is beautifully printed on thick rag paper, bound in a blue paper wrapper. I am not sure that Dobie ever actually read the entire book. He told Al Lowman that "it had quite a bit in it about [Beasley's] sex life" and thus had to be published overseas, and that "there were folks here in Texas who tried their damndest to suppress it."

In fact it has very little in it about Beasley's sex life—she is still a virgin at the end of the book, when she departs for Japan at the age of twenty-seven—but Beasley did repeat some Abilene gossip about the wife of a bank president having an affair with a prominent Baptist minister. The lady's son-in-law became a state legislator, and when the legislature established an un-American activities committee in 1941, Dudley Dobie was hauled before them and questioned about why he had placed a copy of Beasley's un-American book in the University of Texas Library, from which it had been promptly removed.

Although there are some rather frank references to sexual matters in Beasley's book, most of it is about her journey toward refinement and respectability, her intellectual development as a young woman, and her attraction, especially after she moved to Chicago, to socialism, anarchism, and feminism. She describes going to lectures by Margaret Sanger and Emma Goldman, and her involvement in struggles for equal pay for male and female teachers. This, of course, would have been enough to get the book condemned in Texas when it was published, had anyone but a legislator from Abilene and a few book dealers ever read it.

There is a mystery about Gertrude Beasley that has never been solved. In 1989 the Book Club of Texas republished her book, with an afterward by Larry McMurtry. McMurtry, in trying to write a biographical essay about Beasley, hit a blank wall. He could learn nothing about her after she published the book in Paris in 1925. He wrote to every Beasley in the Abilene phone book and received no answers; he wrote to administrators at Hardin-Simmons and received only her enrollment information. As he put it, Beasley "blinked off the radar screen of history" in 1925.

One of McMurtry's letters went to Alice Specht, dean of libraries at Hardin-Simmons. In a 2011 *Texas Observer* article Specht's daughter, Mary Helen Specht, told how the letter motivated her mother and her father, Joe Specht, also a librarian, to embark on a twenty-year-long search for the rest of Gertrude Beasley's story. They found some but not all of it. They learned that she had been deported from England in 1927 after her book had been banned there, and they found a letter that she had written to the Department of State on January 7, 1928, from the ship that was taking her to New York, complaining about her treatment by British authorities and talking about a conspiracy to keep her from publishing a second book she was working on.

In 2000 the 1930 United States census was released, and the Spechts found an entry for a Gertrude Beasley on it, a single woman, born in 1893 in Texas, and a resident in a mental institution in Suffolk County, New York. But there was no way of being absolutely sure that she was the same Gertrude Beasley that the Spechts were tracking, as the New York State authorities would only release information about her to her own family members. In 2008 a grandniece of Gertrude Beasley saw an article about the Spechts' search in the Abilene paper and contacted them for information about her great aunt. Together they were able to obtain a death certificate for the Beasley on the 1930 census. The birth date, birth place, and parents' names matched up, and they learned that she had been committed to the institution ten days after her ship had landed in New York and had lived there twenty-seven years, dying from pancreatic cancer in 1955.

Who had Gertrude Beasley committed, and why? We may never know. The minutes of commitment hearings in New York are not open even to family members. She remains Texas's greatest literary mystery.

March 24, 2016

✣ 23 ✣

TEXAS BRAGS

John Randolph, *Texas Brags*.
Houston: The Anson Jones Press, 1944.

THERE IS NO entry in the *Handbook of Texas* for John Hayward Randolph, nor was he ever elected to the Texas Institute of Letters, but he was a Texas author who probably did more than anyone else in the latter half of the twentieth century to shape the popular conception of Texas. Randolph was the originator of *Texas Brags*, a series of booklets that sold close to a million copies between their first appearance in 1944 and Randolph's death in 1972.

Each edition of *Texas Brags* consisted of sixty-four pages bound in a stiff cardboard wrapper, with each page devoted to a different Texas topic. The booklets were profusely illustrated with colored drawings by Houston artist Mark Storm. The topics included Texas geography, agricultural products, natural resources, demography, history, customs, food, vocabulary, and humor. The tone was boastful ("If all the hogs in Texas were one big hog, he could dig the Panama Canal with three roots and a grunt."), but the statistics were fairly reliable ("There are more sheep in Texas than people in Massachusetts. Over five million of them produce twice as much wool as the next ranking state and nearly 25% of the U.S. total."). The jokes were terrible ("I went to Amarillo but came home broke." "Why?" "I'm a soft touch for Panhandlers."). *Texas Brags* is an abbreviated, lighthearted, and wonderfully illustrated version of *The Texas Almanac*.

The later editions have a self mailer on the back cover that includes this boxed notice: "Postmaster: Take time out for laughs and education. This parcel may be opened for postal inspection whether necessary or not." The 1956 edition has a note on the title page, just above Mark Storm's pen-and-ink drawing of a cowboy saddling his horse, that says, "Published for the enlightenment and entertainment of the world at large." In the 1968 edition, just under the publisher's imprint saying that the book was published by John Randolph Enterprises in Tomball, Texas, are the words, "And to answer the question before it is asked, Tomball is that city north of Buffalo Bayou in whose Metropolitan area lies Houston." Clearly John Randolph had a flippant attitude toward the formalities of publishing.

I got my first copy of *Texas Brags* at the age of seven, a gift from my Fort Worth grandmother, and she sent me a new edition every year all the years that we lived away from Texas. I loved it. It taught me how to be a Texan while living in foreign parts. The inside back covers of the later editions offered merchandise created by Randolph which I had to be restrained by my parents from sending off for: Texas passports, citizenship certificates, flags, and even stock certificates in "a famous Texas oil well."

Several years ago I decided to try to learn more about John Randolph, and I made a small collection of copies of *Texas Brags*, ranging from the first 1944 edition published in Houston by the Anson Jones Press to the "new, revised, Space Age edition" published in Tomball in 1968. The content does not really vary much over twenty-four years. Some of the statistics are updated, and the 1968 edition includes a drawing of the HemisFair tower, but you get the impression that Randolph hit on a good thing in 1944 and stuck with it.

John Randolph proved to be a hard man to learn much about, and I still do not know as much about him as I would like to. In fact, one of the reasons I am writing this column is the hope that someone who does know something about him will read it and get in touch with me. My first clue about him came from the online Library of Congress catalogue, which I was consulting in order to learn how many editions of *Texas Brags* had been published. I noticed an entry there for another book by Randolph called *Marsmen in Burma*. This turned out to be a history of a military unit that Randolph had served in during World War II, an amalgamation of mule-mounted American and Chinese troops called the Mars Task Force that fought in the China-Burma-India Theater in 1944 and 1945.

Then I stumbled on a short article about Randolph in the January 1986 issue of *Texas Monthly* by Terry "Tex" Toler, whom Marfans may remember as the director of tourism for the City of Marfa several years ago. It seems that Toler is also a *Texas Brags* fan and has treasured from childhood a *Texas Brags* map depicting Texas as stretching from the Atlantic to the Pacific coasts and lapping over into Canada and Mexico, one of those items advertised in *Texas Brags* that my parents would not let me buy. Toler had corresponded with Randolph's widow, Ruth Moore Randolph, and had learned that Randolph had conceived *Texas Brags* while stationed in Marfa with the 124th Cavalry Regiment at Fort D. A. Russell in the winter of 1943-1944. The 124th Cavalry was a Texas National Guard unit that Randolph, a Houston advertising man, had joined in 1942 at the age of thirty-four. The regiment was federalized when the war broke out and became the last unit in the United States Army to be mounted on horses. According to Randolph's widow, Randolph was bored stiff with guarding the Mexican border from Marfa and got to thinking about a bus placard advertising campaign he had done for Jax beer before the war, a series of ads he had called "Texas Brags and Drinks Jax Beer." He wrote his wife and asked her to send him his files from that campaign, and the manuscript for the first edition of *Texas Brags* was the result. He worked on it in off-duty hours for four months and sent it to his wife just before his regiment was transferred to Fort

Riley, Kansas, and then shipped to India to become part of the Mars Task Force, charged with clearing the Japanese army off the Burma Road. Before he shipped out he arranged for his Houston friend Mark Storm, a graphic artist for the Humble Oil Company's magazine *The Humble Way*, to do the illustrations, and for the Anson Jones Press to publish the results. By the time he came home from the war in 1945 the first edition had sold 160,000 copies. John Randolph, a native Floridian, was in business promoting Texas for the rest of his life.

August 18, 2016

✣ 24 ✣

BACK TO TEXAS

Bobbie Louise Hawkins, *Back to Texas*.
Berkeley, California: Bear Hug Books, 1977.

BOBBIE LOUISE HAWKINS was a Texas writer that no one thought of as a Texas writer. When she died in Boulder, Colorado, at the age of eighty-seven last month, the headline on her obituary in the *New York Times* described her as "Beat Poet and Author" and only in the ninth paragraph mentioned that she was born in Abilene, Texas. It did say that one of her books was called *Back to Texas*.

Hawkins was the daughter of a teenage mother, Nora Hall, who worked as a waitress and sold vacuum cleaners door to door. She was raised by her mother and stepfather, a plumber named Harold Hall, with the aid of her mother's mother, a tough West Texas woman who was born in 1882 and, according to Hawkins's portrait of her in *Back to Texas*, was about five feet tall, had fourteen children by three husbands and, before she died, twenty-one grandchildren, thirty-one great-grandchildren, and two great-great-grandchildren. One of her maxims was "You don't have to be ashamed of having ignorance or lice, you just have to be ashamed of keeping them." Hawkins said about her, "She was a loving woman."

Hawkins's family moved to Albuquerque when she was ten. As a teenager she started hanging around the Albuquerque Art Center and decided that she wanted to be an artist. She told an interviewer in 2011 that she read all of the time, and that in the books she loved, the people who mattered to her were the artists, so that was what she wanted to be. Shortly after graduating from high school she married a Danish architect, Olaf Hoeck. Hoeck took her to London, where she enrolled in the Slade School of Fine Art, and then to British Honduras, where she taught drawing in several missionary schools. "I went with him because it was an adventure," she said. They divorced, and she returned to Albuquerque, where she met and fell in love with Robert Creeley, a poet who was teaching Latin in a boys' school there. They were together for eighteen years before parting in 1975. Creeley became a distinguished American poet; he dedicated his best-known collection of poems, *For Love*, to Hawkins. Hawkins described Creeley as "the most interesting man I ever met." They parted because of his refusal to accept the fact that she wanted to write, too. Hawkins said that he told her he would never live in a house with a woman who wrote, and that he told friends that there was only room for one writer in a house. After they parted Hawkins became a hero in the feminist movement for her resistance to male dominance. She toured the country in a three-woman show of feminist music, poetry, and prose with Rosalie Sorrels and Terry Garthwaite. She also wrote twenty books.

Back to Texas, published in 1977 by Bear Hug Books in Berkeley, California, grew out of a trip that Hawkins made with her mother shortly after she and Creeley parted. They drove from Albuquerque to Abilene and back, stopping to visit relatives along the way. The book consists of fifty-seven short chapters, none of them more than five or six pages long (one of them is only eleven lines), cast as conversations among Hawkins, her mother, and various relatives. In fact they are conversations. Hawkins told poet and novelist Barbara Henning in a 2011 interview, published in Henning's *Selected Prose of Bobbie Louise Hawkins* (Buffalo, New York: Blazevox Books, 2012) that she took a tape recorder with her on that trip, intending to tape her relatives' conversations. "My relatives, my dear," she told Henning, "were incredible, and it was all because of that habit of sitting around a big kitchen table with a coal oil lamp and telling stories, just passing around the table from one person to the next. That was a major entertainment. Everyone would laugh even if it was the fiftieth time they'd heard this story because it was like a performance." She went on to say that she got the idea of using the tape recorder before she started on the trip, and her plan was that she would listen to all of the tapes when the trip was over and she was back home, and then she would be in the right tempo to start the book. "I thought that if anybody started telling stories I could 'improve' them and put them in the book. That's the first time I registered how good my relatives were as storytellers. All of the stories were unimprovable. They were honed down into something incredible that I just could not improve."

Some of the flavor of *Back to Texas*, the tumble of names and conflicts, slops over into Hawkins's interview with Henning. At one point Henning asks her if she had any trouble with her relatives after the book came out, and Hawkins replies, "My cousin Marilyn came to live briefly in Sausalito with this boyfriend who had sold her a pair of shoes in Lubbock. My mother telephoned and said, 'Marilyn is going to find out about you writing that book, and if she finds out about it, Ollie is going to want a copy, and if you send Ollie a copy, she's going to let Thelma read it and she'll read that part about when Evertt was in the vets hospital, Doris took his money and spent it. So if you send Ollie a copy, will you take that part out?'" Henning's only response is, "That's hilarious."

My favorite story in *Back to Texas* is in the chapter called "When Billy Bob Married," which is about how one of Hawkins's cousins married a sharecropper's daughter, a woman named Alvina. Hawkins describes the house Alvina's parents lived in as "having more rooms than the family had furniture for. . . . You could go into a lanky old room that wouldn't have anything in it but a rocking chair next to a high bare window that looked out on nothing but the horizon." But they did have a table model radio, and when Hank Williams died, Hawkins writes, "Alvina's daddy took the radio out to the woodpile and smashed it up with his axe as a gesture of grief. He said that with Hank dead there wouldn't be any more music worth listening to."

June 28, 2018

✣ 25 ✣

THE OTHER SIDE OF THE TRACKS

Tony Cano, *The Other Side of the Tracks.*
Canutillo, Texas: Reata Press, 2001.

TONY CANO grew up poor in Marfa in the 1950s. His father was a fine cowboy and was a ranch manager on Wayne Cartledge's 9K Ranch on the Texas-New Mexico line, but he was a heavy drinker. Cano's mother left him when Cano was in the first grade, moving to Marfa with her three children and taking a job as a waitress. She had a difficult time making ends meet. In a recent phone interview, Cano told me that sometimes he and his brother would come home from school for lunch and there would be nothing in the house to eat but cornflakes.

Marfa's elementary schools were segregated in the 1950s and, like all Mexican American children, Cano went to Blackwell School. But when he reached the seventh grade he enrolled in Marfa Elementary, the Anglo-American school whose graduates went on to Marfa High School. *The Other Side of the Tracks* grew out of the prejudice that Cano experienced there and at Marfa High, and out of the ways that he and a small group of friends devised to fight it. The novel is about the adventures of a group of Mexican American teenagers who called themselves the Chinglers, a word derived from the Spanish verb *chingar*, which is the equivalent of the four-letter Anglo-Saxon word beginning with *f* that means to have sexual intercourse. The book is a frank and unflinching picture of what it was like to be poor and Mexican

American in Marfa in the 1950s. It should be required reading for every newcomer to Marfa because it explains some of the tensions that still underlie the idyllic images of Marfa and its arts community that have recently appeared in national publications.

The Chinglers broke a taboo by secretly dating Anglo-American girls. Fifty years later, Cano still remembers the sting of that particular prejudice. "You couldn't date Anglo girls," he told me. "You couldn't even talk to them in the hallway. We did it because they told us we couldn't." He told me about one Anglo boy who was in love with a Mexican American girl. He and a Mexican American friend had an arrangement by which they would pick up each other's dates, then meet and exchange girls for the evening, meeting again before taking their respective non-dates home. Another unspoken rule was maintaining a racial balance on high school athletic teams; in the novel a coach is fired for playing an all-Mexican American basketball team, even though it is a spectacularly winning team. Cano puts his finger on the far-reaching ramifications of high school athletics in a small Texas town—something else that some newcomers to Marfa may have a hard time understanding.

The book is more memoir than novel. The ending is somewhat clumsy, and Cano told me that was the only part that did not really happen; all of the other incidents are factual. He said that he cast it as a novel "for legal reasons." When word got out in Marfa that he was writing a book, several people threatened to sue him if he used their names in it, and that put him on guard.

Cano told me that he wrote the novel "as therapy." Even as an adult, he said, he had a lot of anger about the way Mexican Americans were treated in Texas. "Writing the book took a monkey off my back. I learned to put the past behind me," he said. *The Other Side of the Tracks* is not Cano's only book. He and his wife, poet Ann Sochat, have published a Dutch oven cookbook and a book of poems and ranch reminiscences, *Echoes in the Wind.*

Their most recent collaboration was *Bandido*, a biography of Cano's great-grandfather, the revolutionist and bandit Chico Cano. *The Other Side of the Tracks*, however, was a solo effort on Cano's part. He told me that he credits his self-confidence as a writer to two of his Marfa English teachers who saw him as more than a Mexican American troublemaker. "Mrs. Emma Lou Howard taught me how to stand up and talk to a group, and Ms. Mary Lou Kelley made me sit on the front row my senior year and motivated me to do well. If it were not for Ms. Kelley I would not have graduated from high school."

Tony Cano went on from Marfa High to have a career worthy of another book. When he graduated from high school, he told me, his mother gave him sixty-eight dollars and said, "You're a man." He ended up in El Paso, where he got a job working in a Mr. Quick hamburger stand. "When I was twenty-one," he told me, "I said, 'Tony, is this it? Is this what you are going to do the rest of your life?'" He enrolled in Texas Western College, now the University of Texas at El Paso, went on to complete a BA at the University of Missouri, and did graduate work as a teaching assistant at the University of Hawaii.

Cano eventually got into the garment manufacturing business in El Paso and ended up the owner of his own company, Tony Cano Sportswear. Cano's factory became a leading producer of sports jackets for auto racing teams, a narrow but profitable niche. Cano told me that came about because in 1981 he went to Phoenix to see his first auto race. He was impressed by the skill of the drivers, and after the race he went down to congratulate the winner, Bobby Unser. One thing led to another, and he became a regular weekend volunteer on Unser's pit team, eventually being assigned to holding the pit board, the blackboard that tells the driver how many laps he has to go. He designed a set of jackets for the Unser team, and so many other drivers admired them that the next year eight of the thirty-three teams at the Indianapolis 500 were wearing Tony Cano jackets.

Cano is now retired and travels all over the world with his wife. He says that someday he will write a sequel to *The Other Side of the Tracks*, and it will have a happy ending.

December 1, 2011

✣ 26 ✣

SAM HOUSTON'S TEXAS

Sue Flanagan, *Sam Houston's Texas.*
Austin: University of Texas Press, 1964.

SOMETIMES inspiration produced by complete absorption in a subject will result in a superb book, but after the book is published and lauded the author sinks into obscurity. This was exactly what happened with Sue Flanagan's *Sam Houston's Texas*, published in 1964. Flanagan was not a historian, but as a single woman in her mid-thirties she fell in love with Sam Houston, and it shows on every page.

Flanagan was a newspaperwoman, born in San Angelo, Texas, in 1926. She graduated from the University of Denver in 1946, and then spent a year at the New York Institute for Photography, and returned to San Angelo in 1947 with the ability to write limpid sentences and compose beautiful photographs. She had a series of humdrum journalistic jobs for the next eleven years: reporter and photographer at the *San Angelo Standard-Times*; managing editor of the *Sheep and Goat Raisers Magazine*; and public relations person for a furniture store. She did break loose for a year in 1952 when she was awarded a Rotary International scholarship to study English literature at Trinity College in Dublin, Ireland (her father was president of the San Angelo Rotary Club), but when she came home she went back to work for the *Standard-Times*. In 1958 she was serving as volunteer coordinator for the All-Faith Chapel at McKnight Tuberculosis Sanitarium, and she invited Texas

Attorney-General Will Wilson to speak at the dedication of the chapel. Wilson was so impressed by Flanagan that he asked her to come to Austin to join his staff as an administrative aide, and she finally made her break with San Angelo. She later told a friend, "I had to get out of San Angelo because people there kept trying to marry me off and I didn't want to do that."

In 1961, while she was working for Wilson, Flanagan had a chance to examine some original letters written by Sam Houston. The experience transformed her. "I was impressed by his sense of humor," she later told Derro Evans, a reporter for the *Amarillo Globe-Times*. She borrowed Wilson's copy of the eight-volume *Writings of Sam Houston*—the loan lasted three years—and read everything in it, as well as the forty-six published biographies and every contemporary newspaper article about him that she could find. She became obsessed with Houston. She told Evans that she was "drawn to his magnetic personality as a man of vision, an egotist, a man of humor and eloquence." She realized she could use his writings to plot all of his travels across Texas from his arrival in 1832 until his death thirty-one years later, and she started taking weekend trips with her Rolleiflex camera, photographing places he had visited, trying to capture them as they looked when he was there. She soon realized that she had "a bear by the tail," as she told Evans, and arranged to take a nine-month leave of absence from her job. During those nine months she zig-zagged 7,300 miles across Texas following Houston's tracks and shot over one thousand pictures. The result was *Sam Houston's Texas*, published by the University of Texas Press. The book included 113 of Flanagan's black and white photographs, printed by the Meriden Gravure Company, the finest photographic printing company in America.

Sam Houston's Texas received ecstatic reviews. Virginia Gambrell of the Dallas Historical Society, writing in the *Southwestern Historical Quarterly*, called the book "a visual delight," "a real contribution to Texana," and praised "the vast amount of scholarly research [that] went into it." Bill Poole, a crusty professor of history at what is now Texas State University who did not bestow praise lightly, told readers of *Arizona and the West* that it was "an unbelievably beautiful book" which was "a milestone in southwestern history" and that it "must rank among the most remarkable books ever published in the field of Texas history." Exhibitions of Flanagan's photographs were organized at the Amon Carter Museum in Fort Worth, the San Antonio Public Library, and the Daughters of the Republic of Texas Library at the Alamo. Flanagan went on a statewide speaking tour to promote the book. It was so popular that the University of Texas Press reprinted it in 1973.

One immediate result of the publication of *Sam Houston's Texas* was that in 1965 Flanagan was commissioned to do a photographic book on the historic Texas cattle trails north. Her work on that book was interrupted by a special assignment from Governor John Connally, and it did not appear until 1974, under the title *Trailing the Longhorns*, published by the Madrona Press, a small press in Austin. It was not as successful as *Sam Houston's Texas*. Flanagan was not as passionate about longhorns as she was about Sam Houston, and the book was, frankly, dull. It lacked the immediacy of the Sam Houston book. Instead of quoting from the letters and diaries and memoirs of trail drivers Flanagan relied heavily on two secondary sources, Wayne Gard's *Chisholm Trail* and J. Evetts Haley's *Charles Goodnight*, and the reviewers faulted her for that. Her photographs were not well treated by Madrona's printers, the Whitley Company of Austin; they were muddy and murky, and the reviewers pointed that out, too.

By the time the book was published, Flanagan was serving as director of the Sam Houston Memorial Museum in Huntsville, a post to which she was appointed in 1972 and held until her retirement in 1981. She died in San Antonio in 1993.

Flanagan left Texans another legacy besides her two books. Her 1966 assignment from Governor Connally was to help the Texas Tourist Development Agency develop a plan for the exhibit that would represent Texas at HemisFair '68, the San Antonio World's Fair. That exhibit became the Institute of Texan Cultures, now part of the University of Texas at San Antonio. Even though Henderson Shuffler of the University of Texas's Texana Program was appointed as first director of the institute in April 1967, the institute's papers in the Daughters of the Republic of Texas Library in San Antonio show unequivocally that it was Flanagan who conceived the museum's basic program, with its emphasis on the various ethnic groups of Texas and its fifty-six-screen "dome show" that enabled all Texans to find their place in the ethnic mosaic. Her memoranda to Governor Connally reveal her as an astute and meticulous thinker with a clear understanding of the emotional power of exhibitry and imagery. Had she not been a woman, she might well have become the first director of the Institute of Texan Cultures.

March 30, 2017

✣ 27 ✣

A GALLERY OF TEXAS CHARACTERS

Gene Fowler, *Mavericks: A Gallery of Texas Characters.* Austin: University of Texas Press, 2008.

I RECENTLY picked up a book that is so good that I was tempted to lift several chapters from it for my columns. Instead I decided to write a column about it. It is *Mavericks: A Gallery of Texas Characters* by Gene Fowler, published by the University of Texas Press in 2008. *Mavericks* is a book of thirty-four chapters, each chapter dealing with one or more Texas eccentrics. One chapter is about Commodore Basil Muse Hatfield, who devoted the years of the Great Depression to advocating a Trinity River Canal that would make Dallas a leading seaport. Another is on O. T. Nodrog, a bewhiskered resident of Weslaco who combined an interest in flying saucers with the Book of Revelation to proclaim his home the Armageddon Time Ark Base and himself the Earth Coordinator of the Outer Dimensional Forces who would, on the appointed day, effect a six-degree shift in the Earth's axis and turn the Lower Rio Grande Valley into the Garden of Eden. In the meantime, Nodrog sold honey and avocado plants at Weslaco's flea market.

My favorite chapter is about O. L. Nelms, the Dallas millionaire who in the 1950s plastered the city with signs saying "O.L. Nelms Thanks You For Helping Him Make Another Million." Nelms's eccentricity once got me out of a tight spot. One of his daughters is a close friend, and in 1980, when I was working on an exhibit about cowboys for the Library of Congress, I told her that the one thing I needed for the exhibit and could not find was a B-movie cowboy costume from the 1940s, when movie cowboys dressed in semi-military style, wearing pants with piping on the pockets and shirts with rows of buttons on the cuffs.

"I think I have just what you want," she said, and produced a pair of green trousers with white piping on the pockets and down the legs, a gabardine shirt with cactus blossoms embroidered on the yoke, rows of pearl snaps on the cuffs, and a shoulder patch bearing a map of Texas with the letter "T" imposed on it and the words "Texas Trader" underneath, and a pair of green cowboy boots with the red map and "T" motif scattered over the uppers. "These were O.L.'s," she said. "You're welcome to use them in the exhibit."

"What in the world did he do with them?" I asked.

"He wore them on business trips to New York," she said. "People would stop him on the sidewalk there and ask for his autograph."

The author told me that he was somewhat disappointed when the book came out that the reviewers tended to dismiss his subjects as "weird."

"I see them as performance artists," Fowler said, "people on a level with the outsider artists whose work is shown in art galleries. Their lives are their art." Fowler explains this idea in a long introduction to the book, in which he quotes neuropsychologist David Weeks, theater critic Michael Kirby, and performance artist Joseph Beuys.

Gene Fowler is something of a performance artist himself. Although he earns his living as a freelance magazine writer, his roots are in show business. His father was a bandleader who had a theatrical booking company in Dallas, and Fowler's first sniff of greasepaint came when he and two of his high school friends worked as rent-a-hippies, being sent by his father's agency to

Highland Park parties where they recited poetry and strummed on guitars.

Fowler has always been fascinated by the world of vaudeville, circuses, medicine shows, traveling phrenologists, and snake-oil salesmen. In 2002, he and Bill Crawford published a book that combined all of these elements, a history of the radio stations that operated along the Texas-Mexican border in the 1930s, 40s, and 50s, stations with transmitters in Mexico that were so powerful that June Carter supposedly said that you could pick them up with a hairpin from a barbed wire fence in Kansas. The book was a great hit, and he and Crawford turned it into a presentation they called the *Nuevo Vaudeville Documentary Performance*, a two-hour, six-person show with a band that included the music heard on border stations, commercials for Crazy Water Crystals and Hillbilly Flour, and a revival sermon that was a combination of all of the put-one-hand-on-the-radio-and-the-other-hand-on-the-afflicted-part-of-the-body sermons ever heard on the Big X stations, as they were known from their call letters. Fowler's favorite part of the show was letters from historic Texans requesting songs. Davy Crockett, who said he was playing fiddle in a cantina in Chihuahua City, wanted to hear "San Antonio Rose," and East Texas oilman Dad Joiner requested Slim Willet's "Tool Pusher From Snyder."

Crawford has gone on to other interests, but Fowler still does an abbreviated version of this production, called "Border Radio"; when I talked to him a couple of weeks ago he had just returned from Del Rio, where he did it as a one-man show, accompanying himself on the guitar.

Perhaps the most engaging character in *Mavericks* is Henry Ralph Wooley, known as Oil Field Willie or sometimes as Governor Willie, the chief executive of the East Texas oil field. Wooley's specialty was waging mock political campaigns by giving street-corner speeches in double-talk. Wooley appeared in Kilgore in 1931, at the height of the East Texas oil boom, and declared his candidacy against Ma Ferguson for governor in the 1932 election (although he never formally filed). His platform was "ten dollar oil, ten cent beer, bigger dance halls, shorter skirts, and free roses for the ladies." He was immediately adopted by Kilgore's oilmen, who opened accounts for him at local cafes and cigar stands and supplied him with suits and shirts from Kilgore's finest haberdashery, the Hub. Wooley flourished on the sidewalks of Kilgore until his death in an automobile accident in 1940. In his last campaign he ran for an office of his own invention, public suspecter, whose occupant's job was to keep an eye on all public officials. His slogan was "No grifters, no grafters, no insects in the rafters."

Fowler reports that two strangers to Kilgore were listening to one of Wooley's sidewalk orations when one said to the other, "Let's go, he's crazy."

Wooley turned on him and said, "I may be crazy, but you don't see me walking to work in the rain carrying my lunch in a tin syrup bucket." He was a performance artist in spades.

July 24, 2014

✣ 28 ✣

A PLACE IN EL PASO

Gloria Lopez-Stafford, A *Place in El Paso.*
Albuquerque: University of New Mexico Press, 1996.

Occasionally a Spanish-speaking Texan writes a book about his or her life and interactions with Anglo neighbors. These books provide a peek into what I think of as the secret history of Texas, the history that does not get into the textbooks and yet shapes our present. They are valuable not only as part of the historic record but because they are potent tools for intercultural understanding, a very necessary thing in today's world and especially in this country.

My friend Alfredo Gonzales, who grew up in El Paso and is now an antiquarian book dealer in Tucson, recently lent me just such a book, Gloria Lopez-Stafford's A *Place in El Paso,* published in 1996 by the University of New Mexico Press. Lopez-Stafford was born in 1938. Her father was an Anglo who had left his family in South Texas to marry Gloria's much younger Mexican mother. Gloria Lopez-Stafford spent her early childhood in poverty in El Paso's Segundo Barrio, where her father was a dealer in old clothes. Her story is one of successive losses. Her mother died when she was five; her father placed her in the home of a foster mother, an unmarried woman with two grown daughters; her godparents eventually took her out of the Segundo Barrio to live with them and legally adopted her.

A Place in El Paso is raw and bittersweet, but what is clear is how the Segundo Barrio sustained the author as a child. She writes lovingly of its street life, its smells and sounds, of the widows on her block who kept their eyes on the neighborhood children and fixed them mid-morning tortillas and *queso fresco*. In a larger sense the book is about the sustaining Mexican American culture which supported the motherless Gloria. Her Catholic religion was of great importance to her. The parish priest at Sacred Heart Church on Oregon Street, Father Juan Luna, was a constant and consoling presence. Gloria details the calendar of holy days and how and with what special food they were celebrated by her Segundo Barrio neighbors. When a classmate told her how *la llorona* waits by the Franklin Canal, ready to throw passing children into it, Gloria asked her foster mother to bless each of the walls of her bedroom with a prayer every night, so that *la llorona* could not snatch her from her bed.

The Spanish language was an integral part of life in the Segundo Barrio. As a child, Gloria spoke Spanish and was resistant to learning English, even though it was required at school, and she was punished for speaking Spanish there. Her father spoke Spanish at home; she did not realize that he was an Anglo until she moved away from home and heard someone describe him in unflattering terms as such. She describes how her older brother and his friends taught her to memorize the pledge of allegiance to the flag in English. They taught her the first part by having her repeat the words after them, and when she made a mistake they pretended to be a firing squad, blindfolding her in front of a wall and shooting her with raised broomsticks. She soon had the first half down but still stumbled over "one nation, indivisible, with liberty and justice for all," so her brother assigned the other boys to represent the words in the order of their ages. The oldest held a flag and was the indivisible nation, the next was liberty, the next justice, and the youngest, all. Gloria just had to remember how old each boy was, and she got it right in two tries.

Another key concept in the Barrio was *respecto*, respect. The Spanish employed by Gloria's adult neighbors was old-fashioned and polite; words like *estupido* (stupid) were not used. She explains that *dichos* (proverbs) were often employed as a way of commenting on someone's behavior without giving direct offense. Gloria's grandfather Lopez, who was a *curandero*, an herbal healer, knew hundreds of *dichos* and was a master of their deft use. *Respecto* was shown not just among adults but also by children to other children. Children in the Segundo Barrio did not ask each other direct questions that might require embarrassing answers, did not make cutting remarks, and did not push, shove, or yell at each other. Gloria records how shocked she was when she moved from the Segundo Barrio to discover that her new Anglo classmates asked each other any question that came into their heads, and yelled at each other on the playground without causing hard feelings.

The young Gloria was not aware of the fact that some people were prejudiced against Mexicans until she moved with her new parents to Five Points. Her adoptive father, like her real father, was Anglo; her adoptive mother was Mexican, and most of their neighbors were Anglos or Syrians. One day an Anglo classmate told her that she could not come to her house to play because her mother did "not want any Mexican kids around." Gloria at first thought this was some sort of aberration, and then she realized that what she had assumed was just peculiar behavior on the part of some of her classmates was actually prejudice. She learned that being Mexican could be a problem.

A Place in El Paso is not a book about being a victim but about a young girl finding her way to who she is. Lopez-Stafford, who became a professional social worker, recently told me that she was moved to write her book by reading two other books: the anonymous sixteenth-century Spanish picaresque novel *The Fortunes and Adversities of Lazarillo de Tormes*, in which the young hero is apprenticed to a series of masters ranging from a beggar to a bishop; and Harper Lee's *To Kill a Mockingbird*, a coming-of-age novel that evokes a particular time and place. This improbable literary combination is the perfect blend to inspire a Mexican American author.

August 29, 2013

✥ 29 ✥

EXPLORING THE EDGES OF TEXAS

Walt and Isabel Davis, *Exploring the Edges of Texas*. College Station: Texas A&M University Press, 2010.

SIX YEARS AGO Walt and Isabel Davis came to Marfa and visited with their friend Evelyn Luciani. We all had dinner together, and they told me that they were on their way to the Chisos Mountains to find the place where the artist Louis Agassiz Fuertes and his colleagues in the United States Biological Survey, Vernon Bailey and Harry Oberholser, had set up camp in 1901. The Davises were on the first leg of an ambitious retirement project. They were going to drive all of the way around the boundaries of Texas, visiting significant natural history and archaeological sites that had been described by earlier scientists, and then write a book about their adventures. They were inspired, Walt told me, by a trip that *Dallas Morning News* columnist Frank X. Tolbert and his nine-year-old son had made around the borders of Texas when Walt was thirteen years old. Tolbert had phoned in columns about their progress, and Walt had assiduously followed them in the *Morning News*. No two people could have been better qualified to replicate Tolbert's trip. Walt, a wildlife scientist and watercolor artist, had just retired from a long museum career at the Dallas Museum of Natural History and the Panhandle-Plains Historical Museum; Isabel, an enthusiastic birder, had just retired as reference librarian at West Texas A&M University.

The Davises were successful in their search for Fuertes's first campsite. Using copies of two pencil sketches of it that Fuertes had included in a letter to his parents, they were able to find the exact spot using the alignment of ridges and peaks in the sketches with an unusual rock spire. Over the next four years the Davises went on to visit fifteen other sites in border counties from the Gulf Coast to the northeast corner of the Panhandle.

Now, six years later, their book has just been published by Texas A&M University Press. It is called *Exploring the Edges of Texas*, and it is one of the best books about Texas I have read in a long time. Its fifteen chapters, one per site, are illustrated with Walt Davis's watercolor sketches, and each chapter shifts back and forth between the Davises' experiences at the site and those of the scientist who preceded them there, so that the book is not only about the ecological diversity of Texas but about ecological change over time.

Several chapters in the Davises' book will be of particular interest to Far West Texans. The chapter about the Fuertes campsite, "Letters from the Ghost Mountains," describes both the Davises' adventures in the Chisos and those of the US Biological Survey a century earlier, as well as the genesis of one of the most remarkable of all Texas books, Harry Oberholser's *The Bird Life of Texas*. That book had its origins in the report that Oberholser was to write for inclusion in the 1905 report of the Biological Survey's work in Texas, but Oberholser felt that he did not have enough information to publish the report in 1905. He was still working on it when he died in 1963, at the age of ninety-three. By then his manuscript had grown to three million words. Frank Wardlaw, the first director of the University of Texas Press, felt that it still deserved to be published. A Herculean ten-year editing effort, headed by Edgar Kincaid, J. Frank Dobie's nephew and a distinguished birder, managed to distill Oberholser's manuscript into a two-volume, thousand-page book, illustrated with Fuertes's paintings, finally published in 1974 after a seventy-three-year gestation period.

The Davises' chapter "Walking to El Paso" is about their attempt to trace the footsteps of Charles Wright through the Quitman Mountains to Indian Hot Springs. Wright was a botanist who accompanied the 1849 army expedition led by Colonel Albert Sidney Johnston that opened the road from San Antonio to El Paso, passing through the future site of Fort Davis. Wright had expected to be given a wagon for his exclusive use, but at the last minute he was told that wagons were in short supply and he would have to walk the 673 miles to El Paso, which he did. The Davises were able to follow Wright's journey through his letters to the naturalist Asa Gray, which, along with the specimens Wright collected on the journey, are at the Gray Herbarium and Archive at Harvard University. The Davises went to Harvard to read the letters and examine the preserved plant specimens dug from the bank of the Rio Grande so long ago.

A third chapter, "Wild and Scenic River," describes a six-day raft trip the Davises made through the lower canyons of the Rio Grande, following the route of geologist Robert T. Hill and his crew down the river in 1899. I have read Robert T. Hill's journal of that river trip, in a notebook which survived several dunkings in the Rio Grande, and I admire the Davises' perseverance in deciphering Hill's miniscule and water-blurred handwriting. Hill's guide was a beaver trapper named James MacMahon, reputed to be the ugliest man in Texas. The Davises' guide was Taz Besmehin, who was accompanied by her two sisters, Terri and Jean, and the food that they prepared was far better than the rations Hill and his party subsisted on. Walt Davis still remembers their camp cooking. "We ate like royalty," he told me not long ago. Davis said of all of the trips that went into the book, the one he enjoyed most was the one down the Rio Grande. "It was a most intimate experience with the desert," he said. "You were no longer in control. You went where the river went."

Other memorable trips and encounters are recounted, too: visits to spots on the Gulf Coast and the Sulphur and Red and Canadian rivers, and even a canoe trip through downtown Houston via Buffalo Bayou, always in the footsteps of some earlier scientist.

Walt and Isabel Davis are both fine teachers and they know how to arouse the curiosity of readers. Each chapter of this book is a detective story, built around a quest for something.

Exploring the Edges of Texas is a book that will appeal to anyone who is curious about the world around us—and that should include all of us.

July 22, 2011

30

GRAY GHOSTS AND RED RANGERS

Thad Sitton, *Gray Ghosts and Red Rangers: American Hilltop Fox Chasing.* Austin: University of Texas Press, 2010.

When I lived in Fayette County in the 1970s I knew several men whose passion was wolf hunting. This did not mean that they went out with guns to kill wolves. It meant that they kept packs of hound dogs and one or two nights a week they would take the dogs out and stay up all night listening to the dogs chase a wolf through the woods, following the chase in pickup trucks on back roads or, sometimes, sitting around a campfire while the dogs circled around them through the woods.

The wolves that they hunted were actually coyotes, as wolves had been extinct in that part of Texas since the 1930s, but the terminology had clung to the sport long after the wolves had gone. The quarry was not as important as the chase, because the point of the sport was to listen to the music of the dogs baying. An experienced wolf hunter could not only tell which dog was which by the sounds they made, he could tell where the dogs were and how close they were to the coyote, and he could relate that to his fellow-hunters in vivid terms. A wolf hunt was an exercise in translating an auditory experience into a visual one. One of my wolf-hunting friends, Paul Jaster, had a party piece that involved imitating the sounds of a wolf hunt on a harmonica, supplementing the chords of the harmonica with yips and yelps he made with his own mouth and interspersing them with comments like, "now here comes Old Rattler," and "Little Bill's almost got him." He could be persuaded to perform this at barbecues and other outdoor occasions. Hearing him was almost as good as being there by the campfire.

Texas wolf-hunting had its origin in Southern fox chasing, or "hilltopping," as some of its practitioners call it, a sport that was followed all over the South for two centuries but is now almost extinct. Thad Sitton, a Texas historian who has written several good books about backwoods life in East Texas, has recently published a book about hilltopping called *Gray Ghosts and Red Rangers: American Hilltop Fox Chasing* (University of Texas Press, 2010). Reading it has enlightened me considerably about some of the things that I encountered in Fayette County and on forays into East Texas in the 1970s.

Sitton's book is organized into five chapters and an epilogue. One chapter is a history of horseback fox hunting in England and America and an explanation of how it turned into fox chasing in the South in the nineteenth and twentieth centuries, along with descriptions of the types of foxes (red and gray, thus the book's title) and dogs involved. The other chapters describe the techniques, folklore, and demise of the sport. Although Sitton is best-known as an oral historian and has based most of his other books on interviews, much of the material in this book is derived from readers' contributions to three fox chasing magazines, *Red Ranger*, *Chase*, and *Hunter's Horn*. Sitton describes these contributions as "an outpouring of primary sources from forgotten men in nameless communities at the end of the county roads."

One of the magazine contributors frequently quoted by Sitton is Bob Lee Maddux, a Tennessean who raised Walker hounds and published articles about them from the mid-1930s until his death in 1995. Paul Jaster, who had a pack of a dozen Walker hounds, was a great admirer of Maddux. I once introduced Paul to an art museum director from Memphis who was visiting me, and Paul said, "Oh, you're from Memphis. Do you know Bob Lee Maddux?" My visitor said he did not, and Paul was incredulous. "How could you be from Memphis and not know Bob Lee Maddux?" he said. "He's the most famous hound dog man in Tennessee." Paul later warned me to be careful of my visitor; he didn't think the man was from Tennessee at all. "He didn't know who Bob Lee Maddux was," he said.

One topic that Sitton explores is the bond between hunters and their dogs. Gameness, the ability to run all night and not give up the chase, is the quality most valued in a dog, and some hunters consider their gamest dogs extensions of themselves to an uncanny degree. Sitton describes a hunter he knew who, when narrating a chase from the sound of the dogs, would start out using his dog's names—"Big Boy's in Brenham's Woods"—but at a certain point would slip into the first person: "Now I'm crossing Green's Creek. Now I'm in the Ledbetter field." He cites several instances of the reverse phenomenon: dogs that would quit the chase and come into the campfire if their owner went to sleep.

The most interesting and most poignant chapter in Sitton's book is the one in which he describes the decline of fox chasing in the rural South after World War II. He attributes this to the increasing urbanization of the South and the disappearance of the rural landscape, but he focuses in on one aspect of urbanization that would never have occurred to me: the reintroduction of deer into the rural landscape by state fish and game departments to provide recreation for urban hunters. This, he says, led to regulated hunting, perimeter fences, and the erosion of traditional "hunter's rights," meaning the custom of running dogs across other people's property in pursuit of foxes. Fox hounds cannot resist chasing deer, and the reintroduction of deer brought about the "dog wars," confrontations all over the rural South between landowners whose incomes derived from deer-hunting leases and fox chasers, with the landowners threatening to shoot any dogs found on their property. Sitton cites example after example of fox chasers who simply gave up the sport after posted signs had gone up, woven wire fences had appeared in the woods, and their best hounds had been killed. The dog wars were especially intense in East Texas, where I once saw a dog collar pinned up on a bulletin board in a rural general store with a note tacked under it that said, “I will pay $500 for the name of the man who killed this dog.” I knew nothing about fox chasing at the time, but I remember thinking I would not want to be that man.

May 19, 2011

✣ 31 ✣

NEVER THE SAME AGAIN

Jesse Sublett III, *Never the Same Again.*
Berkeley: Boaz Publishing Company, 2004.

MY FORT DAVIS neighbor Stephen Bright once auditioned to play guitar with an Austin punk rock band called the Skunks. "It was in 1979," Bright told me, "and the audition was in a self-storage unit in South Austin that had somehow been wired for electricity. The bandleader was Jesse Sublett, who played the bass guitar. I didn't think he was a trained musician, but he had a beautiful black leather jacket." Bright did not get hired, so perhaps his opinion of Sublett's musicianship was reciprocated. Bright went on to become a well-known classical guitarist and a builder of ten-string guitars. Sublett went on to become one of Texas's most prolific writers, the author of one of the best Texas books I have read in a long time, *Never the Same Again* (Berkeley, California: Boaz Publishing Company, 2004) as well as a series of acclaimed detective novels, a book about the Tim Overton gang and the Austin underworld in the 1960s (*1960s Austin Gangsters*, The History Press, 2015), a history of the Texas Turnpike Authority, numerous screenplays and History Channel television scripts, a slew of articles for *Texas Monthly*, the *Texas Observer*, and the *New York Times*, and a play called *Marathon*. His mystery novels feature a hardboiled detective named Martin Fender who plays bass guitar in a rock band. Sublett is a tough, punchy writer. His writing heroes are Dashiel Hammett, after whom he named his son, and James Ellroy, author of *The Black Dahlia*.

He is also one heck of an editor. He managed to get the manuscript for Eddie Wilson's memoir, *The Armadillo World Headquarters*, into publishable shape when at least two other well-known Texas writers had failed. The "disquieting scent of violence underlying Wilson's narrative" that I mentioned in my column about the memoir several weeks ago is probably due to Sublett's work as coauthor.

Nothing in Sublett's background indicated that he would become a writer. He grew up in Johnson City, a place he described to me as "full of small-minded, racist, red-necked, ignorant people." In high school in the late sixties he had long hair and played the guitar. "I got into a lot of fights just for walking into a room," he told me. He dropped out of Southwest Texas State University after two years in 1974 to move to Austin with his girlfriend, Dianne Roberts, to play music.

In Austin, Sublett and some friends started a band that they called Jellyroll. One Sunday night in August, 1976, the band played a gig in San Antonio, backing up a singer called Queen Bee, and spent the night there. Sublett came home the next day to find that someone had broken into his house and raped and murdered his girlfriend. He was twenty-two years old. After that, he wrote, nothing was ever the same again.

Never the Same Again opens with the story of Dianne Roberts's murder and ends with Sublett's miraculous recovery from throat cancer twenty-seven years later. Neither section makes pleasant reading, at least for a squeamish person like me. The cancer episode includes descriptions of a twelve-and-a-half hour throat surgery that Sublett endured and of the nausea induced by his chemotherapy. I am a person who does not allow my dinner guests to discuss medical matters at the table. But both parts are crisply written, and in between are some wonderful vignettes of life in Austin in the 1970s.

Early in the book Sublett writes about how he and Dianne and some friends attended Lyndon Johnson's funeral in January 1973, stoned to the eyeballs because they had swallowed several bottles of pills they had in the car when a highway patrolman pulled them over on their way to the cemetery at the LBJ ranch. Sublett describes the crunching of fallen pecans under their feet as they walk from their car to the cemetery, and the jittering of mockingbirds in the trees, and the icy cold wind, and Billy Graham's oratory over the casket. I was there that day, too, and I had forgotten how cold it was until I read Sublett's account.

A year and a half after Dianne's murder Sublett started a band called the Skunks, which introduced punk rock to Austin, and some of the best parts of *Never the Same Again* are about the dynamics of life in a band: the long trips in a broken-down van; the petty jealousies and paranoia among the members; the highs of memorable performances; the recognition one received. As Sublett told me, "Being a musician back then was being a member of a special tribe. You went places and people turned their heads. In a truck stop at 5:00 a.m. your table was different from every other table."

The Skunks' home base was a dive on Guadalupe Street called Raul's, which Sublett says was a "funky Tex-Mex joint with cheap wall paneling and plastic plants in baskets hanging from the ceiling." Punk rock was as much about performance art as it was about music, and Sublett has a hilarious description of a concert at Raul's by a rival punk band, the Huns, which opened with the bandleader snarling into the mike, "The Rolling Stones and the Skunks suck! They're boring old farts! They're dinosaurs!" and ended when the Austin police came to tell the band to turn the volume down and the bandleader kissed the officer who had climbed on stage to deliver the message while the guitarist bonked him on the head with his instrument and the audience erupted

JESSE SuBLett

into a sea of fist fights. This went down in Austin music folklore as "Raul's Riot."

Eventually the Skunks achieved the goal of every aspiring rock band: they made an LP record and they played CBGBs in New York, twice, and they became famous. But the most lyrical passages in Sublett's book are those about his wife, Lois Richwine, whom he fell in love with two years after Dianne's murder. They lived together for seven years, married in 1984, and are still together. She has encouraged both his music and his writing. Tellingly, he says that she was the only person he met in the 1970s who spoke lovingly of their parents "without irony or bitterness." It is clear why she is the love of Sublett's life. *Never the Same Again* is about Jesse Sublett, but the heroine is Lois Richwine.

October 12, 2017

32

ARMADILLO WORLD HEADQUARTERS

Eddie Wilson, with Jesse Sublett III,
Armadillo World Headquarters: A Memoir.
Austin: TSSI Publishing, 2017.

EDDIE WILSON says that if he had a larger bladder, the history of Texas music might be different. As Wilson tells the story, one night in July 1970 he was at a South Austin music spot called the Cactus Club listening to the Hub City Movers when he felt the call of nature. There was a long line at the club's restroom, so Wilson stepped outside and found a convenient wall across the alley. The wall was part of an enormous building that had once been a National Guard Armory, and after Wilson zipped up his pants he explored it in the dark and realized that its cavernous spaces would make a perfect music venue. He rounded up some business partners and turned it into Armadillo World Headquarters, an institution that dominated the Texas musical scene for a decade.

Wilson himself has become an Austin institution that has lasted much longer than the Armadillo, and as the proprietor of Threadgill's, a South Austin restaurant with occasional live music, he has been regaling friends and patrons with Armadillo stories for the past forty years. Now he has finally got them down on paper in a beautiful self-published book designed by Lindsay Starr, printed on heavy paper, and illustrated with at least a hundred and fifty black-and-white photographs by the late Burton Wilson and at least as many color reproductions of the famous and eccentric Armadillo World Headquarters posters. The book, *Armadillo World Headquarters: A Memoir*, distributed by the University of Texas Press, is a perfect evocation of a crucial time and place in Texas cultural history. It is also very much Eddie Wilson's own book, with a certain amount of edginess and score-settling in the text and an absolute openness about the illegal substances that fueled the Armadillo's staff and performers and sometimes paid the bills.

The Armadillo World Headquarters opened on August 7, 1970, at 525 ½ Barton Springs Road, and closed on December 31, 1980. Over those ten years it became far more than a concert hall. In Wilson's words, it was "a hippie boot camp, a trade school, a music hall, an art pad, home." It also incorporated a beer garden, a restaurant, a recording studio, a bakery, an ice cream parlor, a jewelry shop, an art gallery, an advertising agency, and a nursery for employees' children. At its peak the Armadillo had 140 full- and part-time employees and countless volunteers and hangers-on.

The Armadillo is best remembered as the place where the fusion between country music and psychedelic rock and roll took place, where Willie Nelson and Waylon Jennings produced what Wilson calls "the cosmic cowboy and progressive country thing," but Wilson is quick to point out that the music presented at the Armadillo was far more diverse than country rock. Over a ten-year period Nelson played there only seven times and Jennings five. Nelson left in 1974 after a dispute with one of Wilson's partners, Bobby Helderman, over the fact that too many of Nelson's entourage carried guns. Emphasizing the diversity of the Armadillo's presentations over the years, Wilson writes, "We had everyone from Shawn Phillips to Slade, and in between we had Frank Zappa, Martin Mull, Bette Midler, Leo Kotke, John McLaughlin and the Mahakrishna Orchestra, and Sonny Terry and Brownie McGhee. . . . We also had ballet every month."

There is plenty in the book for fans of the bands of the 1970s, but in my opinion Wilson is most interesting when he is describing the intricate business arrangements that kept the Armadillo afloat. The advertising agency TYNA/TACI (which was pronounced "teena tacky" and was an acronym for Thought You'd Never Ask/The Austin Consultants, Inc.) was a scheme dreamed up by another partner, entertainment lawyer Mike Tolleson, to get around a state regulation prohibiting beer companies from making contributions to beer retailers. Lone Star Beer paid TYNA/TACI $5,000 a month to promote Lone Star longnecks, and Armadillo artists produced tee shirts, bumper stickers, and posters, including the famous Jim Franklin poster showing a covered wagon inside a Lone Star bottle. The campaign was run by a radio genius named Woody Roberts, who compiled a list of two hundred words that he thought would elicit positive reactions from potential Lone Star customers, had them market-tested by a psychographic research lab in Richardson, Texas, and then commissioned songwriters Bob Livingston and Gary P. Nunn of the Lost Gonzo Band to incorporate as many of the high-scoring words as possible into a song about Lone Star Beer. What emerged was "The Nights Never Get Lonely," recorded by Sonny and the Sunliners, Freddy King, and the Pointer Sisters. And you thought country songs got written by an inspired songwriter just plucking a guitar.

Wilson also describes some seamier business situations, including arguments in the box office over the night's receipts between performers' agents and Armadillo staff members and the tangled relationship between the Armadillo and the television program Austin City Limits. The takeaway is that the music business is a business like any other except that more throats are cut and the egos involved are bigger.

There is a disquieting scent of violence underlying Wilson's narrative, which may have as much to do with Wilson's self-admitted explosive temper as it does with the fact that at bottom the Armadillo was a Texas beer joint. For what it's worth, the Armadillo's security staff took instruction in Zen meditation, and followed the precept of "hug, don't hit," preferring to envelop bad actors in bear hugs and walk them to the door rather than laying them out with punches or blackjacks. Wilson records a couple of stabbings and one fatal shooting, which I guess is not a bad record for a Texas beer joint over a ten-year period.

Wilson left the enterprise in November 1976 after a dispute with his partners over how best to reduce and pay off the business's increasing debt. The Dillo's management was taken over by Hank Alrich, a long-time friend of the house with a private income. Alrich restructured the business's finances and actually had it showing a profit when the landlord, Austin real estate developer M. K. Hage, announced his intention to demolish the building and sell the property. He gave the Armadillo a year's notice, time to organize one hell of a goodbye party on New Year's Eve, 1980. Thirty-seven years later, Eddie Wilson, with the assistance of Jesse Sublett, has recaptured the essence of the place in this fine book. Reading it is not quite the same as being there, but it is as close as you are going to get.

September 21, 2017

33

WATERLOO

Karen Olsson, *Waterloo.*
New York: Farrar, Strauss, and Giroux, 2005.

SOMETIMES works of fiction are as much about places as people; sometimes a novel or a short story can epitomize a city. All of Anne Tyler's books are about Baltimore; most of John P. Marquand's novels are about Boston; John O'Hara's early short stories dissect the social structure of Pottsville, Pennsylvania. Bill Brammer's *The Gay Place* is about Austin, and it is a plangent rendering of the way that city looked and felt in 1960.

I moved to Austin the summer after *The Gay Place* was published, and my friends and I all read it and then spent a great deal of time and energy trying to identify the real people on whom the characters were based (at that age we were not experienced enough to know that most fictional characters are combinations of real people with a big dose of the author's imagination thrown in). The governor, of course, was clearly Lyndon Johnson, whom Brammer had worked for while he was drafting the book. The winsome Ouida, we were certain, was Brammer's ex-wife, Nadine. Willie English, the crusading editor, was clearly Ronnie Dugger, editor of the *Texas Observer.* We knew that the seedy Huggins, a man who could cash checks in a whorehouse, was a state legislator from the brush country named Bob Wheeler because he frequently told us that he was. And we were sure that Roy Sherwood, the legislator who was wooing Ouida, was Bob Eckhardt, a state representative from Houston who eventually married Nadine Brammer.

I got to know Eckhardt pretty well over the next few years because I rented a garage apartment from his mother, a very formidable old lady who was originally a Wurzbach from San Antonio. The apartment was behind the old Eckhardt family home on Rio Grande Street, and when Bob and Nadine Eckhardt came up from Houston for the legislative session in 1965 they stayed in the house. Eckhardt quickly became my hero in Texas politics. Although he affected rumpled seersucker suits, bow ties that were always askew, straw hats, and a broad Southern drawl, he was a New Deal liberal Democrat, a brilliant labor lawyer, and smart as hell. He drove the conservatives who thought all liberal ideas came from New York pinkos crazy because his Texas credentials were impeccable: he was descended on both sides from families who came to Texas in the 1830s; he was related to the King Ranch Klebergs; and his bumper stickers carried a brand that had been used by his family for a hundred years, the initials "EK" over a heart.

Unlike some liberals (I also once knew Ralph Nader), Eckhardt had a whimsical sense of humor and a voracious appetite for life. He was a consummate raconteur and had a fund of Texas political stories that went back to the 1930s. He once told me how, at a Democratic gathering early in 1940, he had been assigned to sign up a South Texas political boss who was known for his iron control over his constituents, mostly poor Hispanics, to support a third term for Franklin Roosevelt. Eckhardt approached the man with a strategy that he thought would appeal to his political interests.

His opening gun was, "Roosevelt's trying to help the poor people."

"Well, so am I," the man said.

"Roosevelt's for the little man," Eckhardt went on.

"So am I," the man nodded enthusiastically.

"Not only that," Eckhardt said, ringing in Hitler and Mussolini, "Roosevelt's against the dictators!"

The boss's eyes narrowed. "What's wrong with dictators?" he said.

Eckhardt went on to serve seven terms in the United States Congress as a representative from Houston. He opposed the Vietnam War and was the author of the War Powers Act, an attempt to limit presidential authority to declare war without the consent of Congress. He was defeated in the conservative sweep that put Ronald Reagan in the White House in 1980, and he came back to Austin to spend his time drinking Scotch and sitting in a treehouse he built behind his house in Clarksville, working on a book he never finished. He died in 2001, at the age of eighty-eight. I went to his memorial service at the House of Representatives in Washington and sat there and wept as his daughter Sarah gave the best eulogy I have ever heard anywhere, far better than the speech Al Gore had made a few minutes earlier.

Now there is a new book about Austin, called *Waterloo,* by Karen Olsson, and Bob Eckhardt's ghost inhabits it in a character called Will Sabert, who dies as the book opens but nevertheless plays a major role in it. Olsson uses Sabert to contrast politicians who believed that they could ameliorate some of life's injustices with politicians who believe in nothing but self-advancement and, by extension, to contrast the Austin that used to be with the sprawling post-tech boom Austin that frustrates me every time I drive over there. The resemblance between Sabert and Eckhardt is far more than superficial. It's clear that Olsson, who was once the editor of the *Texas Observer,* both loves Austin and understands Texas politics.

People will probably describe *Waterloo* as a sequel to *The Gay*

Place, but it's not. It's a funny, sad book about getting older, about being in love, about the increasing meaninglessness of things we once cared about. Most of all, it is a eulogy for a city that may not have ever existed exactly as we remember it, and a book about loving a place even when it changes beyond recognition. It's also the best book about Texas I've read in several years, and I'd say that even if I didn't love the Austin it mourns.

June 15, 2006

34

MAVERICK

Lewis F. Fisher, *Maverick: The American Name That Became a Legend.* San Antonio: Trinity University Press, 2017.

WHAT DOES Samuel Maverick, early San Antonio settler, signer of the Texas Declaration of Independence, and Republic of Texas congressman, have in common with Etienne de Silhouette, Rudolf Diesel, and the Fourth Earl of Sandwich? All four men were responsible for eponyms, nouns that make use of their last names to describe objects. Most Texans know that a maverick is an unbranded calf as well as an unruly individual, but fewer than you might think know who Samuel Maverick was or how his name came to be associated with unbranded cattle. That is why San Antonio historian Lewis F. Fisher begins his delightful book about the meaning of the word maverick, *Maverick: The American Name That Became a Legend*, with a review of all the erroneous stories about Sam Maverick and his cattle. Maverick thought branding was cruel and refused to brand his cattle; he branded every cow he saw and ended up with more cattle than anyone in else in Texas. He was a rancher, a cattle thief, an engineer, the assistant treasurer of the Confederacy. He was a Frenchman, a German, a New Englander, a native of Massachusetts who never left Massachusetts in his life (this last howler from a 1987 article by Maine author John Gould in the *Christian Science Monitor*).

Fisher, who is neither a native Texan nor a Maverick (he came to San Antonio in the Air Force and married a member of the Maverick family), is the author of nine superb books about the history of San Antonio. In *Maverick* he has produced a thoroughly researched account of Sam Maverick's life and his acquisition of the cattle herd that went unbranded, possibly the first time that the full and correct story has ever appeared in print. As Fisher tells the story, Maverick, who was born in Pendleton, South Carolina, in 1803, first came to Texas in 1835 and bought land on Lavaca Bay and in San Antonio. He eventually settled permanently in San Antonio and before his death in 1870 acquired three hundred thousand acres of land scattered all over Texas. In 1847 he bought 450 cattle and a five-hundred-acre farm on the Matagorda Peninsula from a man named James Tilton. This is an important point because earlier writers on the subject, even Sam Maverick's son George, have stated that Maverick had no interest in ranching and only took the Matagorda cattle to settle a debt. Fisher found the bill of sale for them in the Maverick Family Papers at the University of Texas at Austin, and there is a picture of it in the book.

Maverick put the farm and the cattle in charge of an enslaved African American named Jack, and Jack neglected to brand the annual calf crop, so after a few years the unbranded calves were wandering all over the Matagorda Peninsula. In 1854 Maverick decided to move his herd to his Conquista ranch on the San Antonio River. He bought 150 more head before taking the cattle off of the peninsula, and when they reached the Conquista he once more put Jack in charge of the cattle, and once more Jack failed to brand any of them. A few years later Maverick sold his Conquista herd to a neighboring rancher, Augustine Toutant-Beauregard, and as Toutant-Beauregard's cowboys set out to round up the newly purchased cattle they spread the word that any unbranded cattle on the range were Maverick's, and the word quickly entered the language of the Southwest. Its first appearance in print was in a San Antonio newspaper in 1867 and the first erroneous story concerning its origin (it identified Sam Maverick as "a wealthy and influential German") appeared in the *St. Louis Republican* a few months later. People have been getting it wrong ever since.

"Maverick," which Fisher describes as "a shape-changer," soon morphed into an adjective and then a verb, and its meaning expanded to mean masterless people as well as masterless cattle. Fisher tells the story of the expansion with skill, humor, and scholarship. It involves journalists, lexicographers, Grover Cleveland, Teddy Roosevelt, and of course the incomparable New Deal congressman from San Antonio, Maury Maverick, Sr., who contributed his own word, gobbledygook, to the English language, but that tale is only half of the book.

The other half is the amazing story of the increasing popularity of the word in the second half of the twentieth century. Fisher attributes this phenomenon to the introduction of the television series *Maverick: Legend of the West* in 1957 and the Ford Motor Company's use of the name for an automobile from 1969 to 1979. The television series was written by Roy Huggins, who named his lead character, Bret Maverick, a card-playing grafter, after Samuel Maverick and Huggins's son, Bret. There seem to be no records describing how the Ford Maverick was named, but its radiator badge was a Longhorn head. Fisher cites a Ford brochure describing the 1969 model that reads, "Why do you call it a Maverick? Because it is unlike any other car. . . . A maverick is different. It breaks the rules. And Ford's Maverick breaks them in your favor." Ford presented the first Maverick off the assembly line to Sam Maverick's last surviving grandson, seventy-nine-year old James Slayden Maverick of San Antonio.

By a creative use of Google, Fisher has tracked the use of the word as a brand name, and has compiled a long list of improbable uses, ranging from steak houses (well, maybe not too improbable) to sports teams to skin-care products to watches, wine, beer, flower seeds, pet food, furniture, popcorn in South Africa, and motorcycles in Argentina. He has even found hotels in Siberia and Bulgaria named Maverick.

His most astonishing discovery, he told me, was that the name of the Apple computer program OXS Maverick was a fifth-generation descendant of his wife, Mary's, great-great-grandfather, Sam Maverick. In 2012 Apple decided to use place names in California for its computer programs, and the Maverick program was named after a place in Half Moon Bay south of San Francisco, well-known to surfers, called Mavericks Point. Mavericks Point was named for the occasional one-hundred-foot high waves that occur there, which were first observed by a trio of surfers in 1961. The surfers called the waves Mavericks after a German Shepherd belonging to one of them, who liked to paddle out with them and frolic in the waves. The dog was named after the hero of the Maverick TV series, who in turn was named for Sam Maverick.

What do you suppose old Sam Maverick would think about being the namesake of a computer program?

February 1, 2018

✣ 35 ✣

COMFORT AND GLORY

Katherine Jean Adams, *Comfort and Glory: Two Centuries of American Quilts from the Briscoe Center.* Austin: University of Texas Press, 2016.

THIS IS THE TIME of year when heavy boxes full of new books about Texas arrive at my house because I serve as a judge in several state-wide book contests. This year's boxes included an outstanding book about quilts, Katherine Jean Adams's *Comfort and Glory: Two Centuries of American Quilts from the Briscoe Center,* just out from the University of Texas Press. It illustrates 115 quilts from the University's Winedale Quilt Collection and includes 115 well-researched essays, one for each quilt. The essays were written by Adams, who has been working with Briscoe Center's quilt collection since 1995.

This remarkable collection, housed at the University of Texas at Austin's Briscoe Center for American History, originated with seventeen nineteenth-century American quilts donated by Houston collector and philanthropist Ima Hogg to the University's Winedale Historical Center in 1966. I became the curator of that collection in 1970, and I remember rolling those quilts on acid-free paper cores and wrapping them with linen to protect them from exposure to sunlight and mud-daubers, much to Miss Ima's displeasure—she wanted all of them to remain continually on view. The collection has now grown to over 500 quilts, many of them with Texas associations. Adams has winkled out the histories of most of them, and her essays make fascinating reading.

A typical entry is the one on page 103 about Amanda Hammonds's Lone Star quilt, which she made at the age of eighteen in 1858 while living with her parents and siblings in Rusk County, Texas. The quilt is striking: an assertive red star on a white field framed by fourteen square borders in red, white, and blue. The quilt is trimmed on two sides by an outer border of curved stems, leaves, and berries; the other two sides are bare.

Adams's research revealed that after the Civil War, Amanda and her husband, George Linn, joined a group of Texans who formed a colony in Brazil. The quilt went to Brazil with them, was shipwrecked with them off the coast of Cuba, was salvaged, and continued to Brazil and returned to Texas with them when, disillusioned, they came home and settled in Navarro County.

The quilt passed to Amanda's daughter Daisy when Amanda died in 1909, and Daisy and her husband took it with them when they moved to Los Angeles in the nineteen-teens. In 1946 the widowed and childless Daisy decided to return her mother's quilt to Texas. She packaged it up and mailed it to Governor Coke Stevenson, who turned it over to the Texas Memorial Museum, whence it came to the Briscoe Center.

Now here is the kicker. One edge of the quilt has been repaired by being stitched up on a primitive sewing machine. Adams's research turned up a list of the colonists who accompanied the Linns to Brazil, compiled by one of the colonists. The Linns are on the list, and then at the bottom the writer added this note: "I remember three more names. Sailor Smith and Mr. Croney and an old maid. I forget her name but she had had a sewing machine, the first I ever saw. She was with the Linns I think." Adams is reasonably sure that it was the old maid's sewing machine that repaired the Linn's quilt, and she includes a photograph of a portable hand-powered sewing machine from the 1860s with the entry.

Quilts can be made in timeless patterns, but they can also exemplify the times in which they were made. Amanda Hammonds's Lone Star quilt expresses the optimism of the young state, only recently an independent republic. Effie Roe's tobacco sack quilt on page 232 is the perfect metaphor for the hard times of the Depression. Roe, who lived on a farm in Bastrop County, did not have enough money to buy cloth for a quilt, but someone in her family bought tobacco. Roe made a quilt by stitching together 576 cotton Bull Durham tobacco sacks, each one measuring 2 ½ by 3 ½ inches. Before piecing them together she took the drawstring out of each one, washed the sack, dyed it brown, blue, gold, or green, and stuffed it with cotton.

Minnie Rucker of Franklin, Texas, celebrated the nomination of Franklin D. Roosevelt and his running mate, John Nance Garner of Texas, in the summer of 1932 by making the quilt pictured on page 180. It has an eight-pointed red, white, and blue star in the center, surmounted by the embroidered words "The Eyes of Texas Are Upon You." Below the star are the additional words "Garner 1932 Democrats Roosevelt." Their order leaves no doubt about who the motto was pointed at. According to Adams's research, Rucker mailed the quilt to the new vice president the day after the election, and Garner instructed his wife to write her a thank you letter, which was published in the Franklin newspaper.

In a few cases the documentation for a quilt is beyond Adams's reach. A red and white quilt in a pattern known as Burgoyne Surrounded, pictured on page 58, came to the collection from the descendant of a family that once owned a plantation in Louisiana, where the quilt was supposedly made before the Civil War. The donor told Adams that her grandmother had a trunk full of letters, business records, and household accounts from that plantation, which she remembered reading when she was in high school, but that another family member had subsequently used them to make art collages, and exposure to sunlight had rendered them unreadable.

Adams's book also provides an insight into the world of late twentieth-century quilters and collectors, the founders of the modern quilting revival. The Briscoe Center has acquired not only quilts but the papers and libraries of several modern quilt enthusiasts, including Kathleen H. McCrady of Austin, known for the Quilt History Study Halls she held in her backyard studio, and Joyce Gross of Mill Valley, California, long-time publisher of the *Quilters' Journal* and one of the organizers of the American Quilt Study Group. The Gross collection at the Briscoe includes 170 quilts, including one pictured on page 182 made in the 1930s by a Prescott, Arizona, woman named Emma Andres. According to Adams's essay, Andres worked in her father's cigar store until his death, and then she turned the store into the Happiness Museum, where she displayed her quilts. That's a museum I'd like to visit.

February 9, 2017

✣ 36 ✣

RINGSIDE SEAT TO A REVOLUTION

David Dorado Romo, *Ringside Seat to a Revolution: An Underground Cultural History of El Paso and Juárez, 1893-1923.* El Paso: Cinco Puntos Press, 2005.

DAVID ROMO is a man of many parts. He is a psychogeographer, a microhistorian, and the grand-nephew of a saint. I had lunch with him the other day in El Paso because I was interested in a book he has just published called *Ringside Seat to a Revolution,* and I learned a little bit about these matters as well as a lot about the side effects of the Mexican Revolution of 1910-1930 on Romo's hometown of El Paso, which is the topic of his book.

I'll start with psychogeography. This, Romo explained, is a technique of observing and recording a city's essences by taking randomly motivated walks through it. It was developed by a now obscure group of French artists and anarchists who called themselves the Situationist International and flourished between 1957 and 1972. Romo is exactly the kind of fellow who would know about the Situationist International. The ultimate literary expression of psychogeography is a novel by Paul Auster called *Cities of Glass,* in which a detective follows a suspect on his daily walks around New York. When the detective plots the walks on a city map, he finds that their routes spell out the words "Tower of Babel." Romo's own strolls around El Paso and Juarez, and through those cities' twin pasts, did not spell anything out, but they led him to some very strange people.

Microhistory is a way of doing history that has become increasingly popular over the last thirty years. While ordinary historians try to understand the past through big events like wars and political movements, the microhistorian looks at the past on a very small scale and focuses on the doings of a group of ordinary people who live in a constricted area, like a seventeenth-century Chinese village or a Paris neighborhood during the French Revolution. Their theory is that small and sometimes offbeat doings can illuminate a whole culture. Romo's Chinese village is the back streets and seedier neighborhoods of El Paso and Juarez, with their bars and jazz clubs full of soldiers of fortune and their tiny printing shops churning out revolutionary manifestos, and his book chronicles plenty of offbeat doings.

Ringside Seat to a Revolution takes its title from the fact that many El Pasoans treated the Mexican Revolution, and particularly the several battles in which the neighboring city of Juarez changed hands, as a spectacle to be observed from their rooftops. In fact, for several years the Paso del Norte Hotel advertised that it was "the only hotel in the world with a view of a Mexican Revolution." Romo's view of the revolution, however, is far more intimate, and it focuses on the peculiar currents that flowed back and forth across the border and the characters that they carried with them. One chapter, for instance, is about Teresita Urrera, faith healer and inspirer of revolutionaries. Another outlines the career of El Paso journalist Victor Ochoa, who thought that revolution was a form of astral projection and invented flying machines in his spare time. A third is about the difficulties of shooting films on the border during the revolution—one gringo director is quoted as saying that what the revolution needed was "a director and a scriptwriter." Every chapter is illustrated with wonderful photographs and is permeated with Romo's finely honed sense of the absurd.

A scholarly looking man in his late thirties or early forties, Romo grew up in El Paso and went to Stanford, where he majored in Judaic studies. "But all you can do with that," he told me, "is to be a philosopher or teach chess." He did in fact once teach chess in the El Paso public schools. He also spent five years in Florence, Italy, where he worked in experimental theatre and had a radio program. He is fluent in Spanish, English, Hebrew, and Italian, reads classical Greek, and is working right now on learning Tarahumara. Above all, he says, he is a research fanatic, and he spent five years plowing through archives scattered from the Getty Research Institute in Los Angeles to the Smithsonian in Washington to write *Ringside Seat to a Revolution.*

Over lunch Romo told me that one of his great-uncles was a priest named Toribio Romo, who was murdered in Mexico during the Cristero War in the 1920s and was canonized by Pope John Paul II as one of the Martyrs of Mexico. He is known in California and Arizona as *el santo pollero*—the holy alien-smuggler—because he sometimes appears to illegal immigrants and helps them safely across the border. This has nothing to do with Romo's book. I just thought I'd mention it because I've never had lunch with a saint's grand-nephew before.

November 10, 2005

37

HENRY COHEN

Jimmy Kessler, *Henry Cohen: The Life of a Frontier Rabbi.* Austin: Eakin Press, 1997.

I WAS IN Galveston several weeks ago for the annual meeting of the Philosophical Society of Texas, and I ran into Jimmy Kessler, who is one of the most entertaining men in Texas as well as a leading historian of Jewish life in the state. Kessler is the rabbi of Congregation B'nai Israel in Galveston, which is the oldest Reform Jewish congregation in Texas. He gave everyone at the meeting a copy of a little book that he has written about one of his predecessors, entitled *Henry Cohen, The Life of a Frontier Rabbi.* Cohen, who was the rabbi of B'Nai Israel for sixty-two years, was one of the most remarkable of twentieth-century Texans, although he certainly did not look like a stereotypical Texan. In fact, he looked a good deal like Jimmy Kessler. He was a short, prematurely bald man with a heavy brush moustache, and in his prime he affected a frock coat, a white bow tie, and a white shirt with detachable cuffs, which he regularly covered with penciled telephone numbers and notes about meetings. He had the air of an absent-minded professor about him. But President Woodrow Wilson once called him "the foremost citizen of Texas."

Rabbi Cohen was born in the London ghetto in 1863, and he never forgot what it was like to be poor and to be discriminated against. What made him remarkable was his dedication to humanitarianism and the fact that he extended that dedication far beyond

Galveston's Jewish community. Although Cohen came to Galveston in 1888 and died in 1952, Galvestonians still tell each other stories about him, and many of those stories are in Kessler's book. The rabbi was a tireless hospital visitor, and, unlike Galveston's Protestant ministers, he did not confine his visits to members of his own flock. He was fond of saying that there was no such thing as Episcopalian scarlet fever, Catholic arthritis, or Jewish mumps. Many elderly Galvestonians of all faiths have stories about waking up in a hospital room to find the dapper rabbi sitting by their bed, ready to cheer them up with jokes and stories.

One of the long-lasting legends about Cohen concerns his trip to Washington on behalf of a Russian boilermaker who had arrived in Galveston as a stowaway on a freighter. He had no papers, and the local immigration authorities were about to deport him back to Russia, where he was wanted by the Czar's police for revolutionary activities and would have been imprisoned if not executed. Cohen heard about his plight and went to the immigration office to plead for his release, but to no avail. Cohen then borrowed $100 and took a train to Washington, where he went to Senator Charles Culberson's office on the man's behalf. Culberson declined to intervene, but as a courtesy he arranged an appointment for Cohen with President William Howard Taft. When Cohen got into Taft's office, he made his pitch for the Russian. Taft politely explained that it would not be good policy for the president to interfere in an immigration matter, but added that he was impressed that the rabbi would travel so far to try to help a fellow Jew. "The man is not Jewish," said Cohen. "He is a Greek Catholic. But he is a human being." Taft was so moved, according to the story, that he ordered that the man be released immediately.

Cohen's best friend in Galveston was Father James Kirwin, the Catholic rector of St. Mary's Cathedral. They were a Mutt and Jeff pair—Cohen was five feet one inch tall, and Kirwin was over six feet—but they shared a sense of humor and a hatred of prejudice. In the early 1920s the Ku Klux Klan tried to organize a klavern in Galveston, which had large Catholic and African American populations. A group of Klansmen from the mainland announced their intention to drive over the causeway to the island and parade down The Strand, Galveston's main street. The causeway was quite narrow, and Rabbi Cohen and Father Kirwin decided to thwart them by taking their cars out onto the causeway and turning them across it. They were accompanied by the county sheriff and a group of armed deputies who were determined to see that no harm came to the clergymen. When the Klansmen encountered the parked cars and the deputies they demanded that the sheriff let them by. The sheriff replied that he and his men were only trying to help the rabbi and the priest with their car trouble, but unfortunately they hadn't been able to get the cars started and so the causeway was closed. The Klan never came back.

Between 1907 and 1914 Cohen acted as the Galveston agent of the Jewish Immigrant Information Bureau, an organization established by financier Jacob Schiff of New York to settle Russian and Eastern European Jews in the Southwest and Midwest. Cohen met the immigrant ships when they arrived in Galveston and helped the newly arrived families reach homes in communities as far away as Fargo, North Dakota. Because of cheap railroad fares, many settled in the East Texas communities of Marshall, Tyler, Texarkana, and Palestine, and today those towns are full of people who have fond family stories about Rabbi Cohen of Galveston. He is remembered far beyond his congregation and far beyond Galveston.

January 26, 2006

38

TÍO COWBOY

Ricardo D. Palacios, *Tío Cowboy: Juan Salinas, Rodeo Roper and Horseman.* College Station: Texas A&M University Press, 2007.

NOT LONG AGO my friend Jim Bratcher of Bulverde recommended a book called *Tío Cowboy* to me. Bratcher is an old Fort Worth boy who grew up on the North Side and worked in the stockyards when he was a kid. He has been a professor of English at several universities as well as a professional horse-breaker, and his interests range from the poetry of T. S. Eliot to the history of saddles. He has kept up an active scholarly life in retirement, contributing reviews and articles regularly to several journals. He is also a self-proclaimed curmudgeon who does not suffer fools gladly or in fact at all, and I have learned through our fifty years of friendship that when he says a book is good there is not one tin word in it.

So when he suggested that I read *Tio Cowboy* I ordered a copy from Texas A&M Press, and as usual he was right. It is good. It is the biography of Rodeo Hall of Fame roper Juan Salinas, written by his nephew Ricardo D. Palacios, a Laredo lawyer. But it is more than a biography. It is a sharp insight into life on the ranches of the South Texas brush country, where Salinas grew up and ranched until his death at ninety-four, and on the national rodeo circuit in the 1930s and 40s, where he made his name as a roper. Juan Salinas was born in 1901 on the fourteen-thousand-acre Las

Blancas Ranch, in Webb County about forty-five miles northeast of Laredo. His father, Antonio Salinas, was a direct descendent of Captain Tomas Sanchez, the founder of Laredo, and part of a small group of landowning Hispanic families who controlled politics and social life in Webb County. According to the author, these families produced males who were confident, independent, rambunctious, and contrarian, and this description fits both Antonio Salinas and his son Juan. Antonio Salinas, a Webb County political leader, took a bullet in the abdomen in the infamous Laredo election riot of 1888 and later served as sheriff of Webb County. He did not get around to marrying Juan's Anglo mother until they had four children together. Juan grew up in a horse culture that took shape in Spain and Mexico and was brought to South Texas in the late 1700s: males rode, raced, and roped from fine horses before they reached puberty. Being an accomplished horseman was synonymous with being a man.

When Juan Salinas was in his late teens, his father sold the Las Blancas ranch and bought another closer to Laredo, near the community of Encinal, and when Antonio Salinas died in 1923 Juan inherited a portion of that ranch, which he operated for the rest of his life, raising cattle and horses. In 1925 Juan and his brother Tony started hitting the weekend rodeo circuit in Texas, roping calves in Corpus Christi, Del Rio, San Antonio, Junction, San Angelo, Houston, Beaumont, Fort Worth, and Dallas, as well as in the small South Texas towns near Laredo. Some of these events were full-blown rodeos with prize money made up from the entry fees; others were simply match ropings, in which the contestants bet on themselves. Sometimes the stakes were pretty high; at one match roping in Uvalde in the early '30s Salinas walked away with $15,000. His opponent was Toots Mansfield, who was named National Calf-Roping Champion seven times between 1939 and 1950. Salinas never beat Mansfield again, but they remained friends for the rest of their lives, and Salinas once gave Mansfield a horse, which creates a special bond between horsemen. It was on the Texas rodeo circuit that Salinas met his wife, Bertha Hargraves of Beaumont. They were married in 1936.

That same year Salinas decided to go on the national rodeo circuit. He teamed up with two other South Texas cowboys, and they set out in a new Chevrolet on a tour that took them to Frontier Days in Cheyenne, the Pendleton Round-Up, the Calgary Stampede, the World Championship Rodeo in Madison Square Garden, and a lot of stops in between. Salinas later said that his primary motive in undertaking this tour was money. He was paying the cowboys on his ranch a dollar a day, and he had to get it somewhere. Salinas stayed on the national circuit for ten years, the only Hispanic in the top money circles, finally retiring in 1946 at the age of forty-five. He continued to run a successful ranching operation at Encinal for the next forty-five years, surrounded by his trophies and his prize saddles and occasionally hosting a roping at the ranch arena.

The book's author, Ricardo Palacios, gathered much of the material for this book while caring for his uncle in Salinas's declining years, driving him around the ranch and listening to his stories. Salinas told his nephew that even though he was the only Hispanic in national professional rodeo at the time, he never encountered racism on the national circuit. He did remember that once at a Texas roping a man in the stands shouted something about a "damn Mexican" when Salinas entered the arena. Salinas's Anglo wife, Bertha, who happened to be sitting behind the heckler, broke a beer bottle over his head. As Palacios puts it, "Word got around, and soon everyone knew that you did not say anything negative about Tío Juan if you were sitting near Tía Bertha."

Most of the stories are not so violent. One of the best has to do with an old horse named Fundillo that Salinas bought for his wife to ride. Now, fundillo in border Spanish means backside or butt. At ranch parties, a time would come when everybody wanted to go riding. Salinas would wait until a crowd had gathered and then shout to one of the ranch hands, "*Anda agárrale el fundillo a Berta*" ("Go grab Bertha's butt"), meaning, of course, go get her horse. This became a standard family joke, and every time Salinas used that phrase to call for his wife's horse everyone laughed as though it was the first time they had had ever heard it.

I imagine that Salinas had polished many of the stories in this book before his nephew heard them and wrote them down, because the text has the quality of a well-worn saddle or a comfortable pair of boots. It is a fine book, and I'm grateful to Jim Bratcher for suggesting it to me. I'll bet many of my Big Bend neighbors would enjoy it, too.

November 1, 2007

✣ 39 ✣

THE WORLD WAR I DIARY OF JOSÉ DE LA LUZ SÁENZ

Emilio Zamora, *The World War I Diary of José de la Luz Sáenz.*
Texas A&M University Press, 2014.

THE FIRST Veterans Day was celebrated ninety-seven years ago on November 11, 1919. It was called Armistice Day back then, and it marked the first anniversary of the armistice that brought an end to what the generation that went through it called the Great War or the World War. That war was truly a world war. Men from Kent and Lincolnshire died in Mesopotamia and East Africa; soldiers from New Zealand and Australia fought on Turkish beaches; Chinese labor battalions dug trenches in France; a Brazilian naval squadron sank German U-boats in the Atlantic Ocean; boys from Kansas faced Germans in France and Belgium and marched across Siberia. The machine gun, trench warfare, and the armored tank made it a war of unprecedented horror. When it was over, seventeen million people had died. In the United Kingdom, Canada, and the other Commonwealth nations, November 11 is known as Remembrance Day in honor of those dead.

Even though the United States did not enter the war until April 6, 1917, when the fighting had been going on for two and a half years, two million young Americans went to Europe with the American Expeditionary Force, and 116,500 of them died there.

One of the men who went and came back home was José de la Luz Sáenz of Realitos, Texas. I can think of no better way to celebrate Veterans Day than to pick up his book about his experiences in the war, which has been recently translated and edited by Dr. Emilio Zamora of the University of Texas at Austin and published by Texas A&M University Press under the title *The World War I Diary of José de la Luz Sáenz*. It is the only World War I diary published by a Mexican American doughboy.

Sáenz, who was a schoolteacher, was drafted into the army in February 1918 and served as a private in the 360th Infantry Regiment of the Ninetieth Division until June 1919. He saw combat in France and was part of the Army of Occupation in Germany after the armistice. His diary was first published in Spanish in 1933 by Artes Gráficas Press in San Antonio under the title *Los méxico-americanos en la Gran Guerra*. According to Dr. Zamora, Sáenz published the book because he had become a political activist, joining the battle for Mexican American civil rights, and he thought that a record of the valor of Mexican Americans from Texas in the Great War would further that cause.

Sáenz was thirty years old, a married man with children, when he embarked on the greatest adventure of his life. He was also an intellectual with a keen sense of the injustices that he had experienced as a Mexican American in South Texas and would continue to experience in the army. He describes in somewhat formal prose how his regiment, largely made up of men from Texas and Oklahoma, trained at Camp Travis in San Antonio, travelled by train to New York, and crossed the Atlantic on the troopship *Olympic*. As a teacher and an older man, Sáenz had a well-developed sense of self-worth, and he frequently records incidents of insults and discrimination from "rude and uneducated" Anglo non-coms and officers. In training and on the voyage to France, Sáenz found solace in the companionship of other Mexican Americans in his regiment, whom he referred to as "we Aztecs."

They looked up to him, and he was able to write letters home in Spanish and English for those who were illiterate.

Once in France, Sáenz set about teaching himself French, and by conversing with French soldiers and civilians and reading French newspapers he quickly became fluent in the language. He was much in demand among his fellow soldiers as a translator of French newspapers, the only source of war news available. His ability as a translator may have saved his life.

As he tells it, his regiment, after several months behind the lines, had just taken its place in the trenches when a messenger told him that the colonel wanted him. He went back to regimental headquarters, a dugout thirty feet underground and a half-mile behind the front line, where he found Colonel Howard Price holding a sheaf of telegrams in French. Price asked Sáenz to read them to him in English and then type them up, and when he did so Price ordered him to remain with the regimental headquarters as a translator and typist rather than returning to his front-line company. Recording this assignment, he writes, "I can see that I will now use this typewriter as a weapon to battle the subjects of William II." Sáenz witnessed plenty of combat and experienced some heavy shelling, but he did so from a relatively safe shelter.

He continued to consort with his Tejano buddies. In one touching passage he describes how he cooked breakfast with Eduardo Barrera from San Diego and Eulogio Gomez from Brackettville, saying, "The only thing Barrera missed in the breakfast we gave him was the chilipitin peppers from Tío Quemado Creek in Duval County." In another passage he records how three of his friends were killed by a German shell when, against orders, they left their trench to gather grapes in a nearby vineyard. He writes, "The whole world trembled when someone mentioned the German artillery. . . . The Mexicans were the only ones who dared to mock the despicable Boches."

After the November 11 armistice, Sáenz's regiment marched across Luxembourg and into Germany, setting up camp at the town of Zeltingen, near Trier, and remaining there as part of the Army of Occupation until May 1919. In camp Sáenz began teaching night classes in English for Mexican American soldiers, and at the approach of Lent he organized a Mexican-style Carnival celebration that was attended by fifty Tejanos, whose names he gives. The list includes Juan Monjares from Fort Davis and Fidel Gleim from Shafter.

José de la Luz Sáenz returned to the States unscathed, but his experiences in the war, and those of his Mexican American comrades, sharpened his desire to fight for social justice at home. For a while he entertained the idea of establishing a utopian colony of Mexican American veterans on the banks of the Nueces, where a corps of community leaders would be trained. In the late 1920s he became active in the League of United Latin American Citizens and remained a member until his death in 1953, continuing the battle against discrimination that he had started at Camp Travis in 1918. He was a fighter for democracy at home as well as in France.

November 10, 2016

✣ 40 ✣

TEXAS CATTLE BRANDS

A.J. Ford, *Texas Cattle Brands: A Catalog of the Texas Centennial Exposition Exhibit.* Dallas: Clyde C. Cockrell Company, 1936.

IN THE LATE 1970s I had a job that was a Texas historian's dream. I was the curator of history at the Dallas Historical Society, in charge of a collection of some ten thousand objects relating to Texas history. The collection, which included Santa Anna's spurs and Fannin's watch—the one he gave to a Mexican officer before he was executed at Goliad—had been put together in the early 1930s by the director of historical exhibits for the 1936 Texas Centennial celebration, Dr. Herbert P. Gambrell. After the Centennial Exposition closed, the Dallas Historical Society ended up with the collection; the building it was exhibited in, a magnificent Art Deco structure called the Hall of State; and with Dr. Gambrell, who remained as director of the Society until shortly before I went to work there.

Gambrell had a unique collecting method. When the planning for the Centennial began, he ran advertisements in every newspaper in Texas announcing a "relic contest." The advertisements asked schoolchildren to talk to their grandparents and find out if they had anything in their possession that had been used in Texas before 1845. If they did, the children were to submit a drawing of it and a short essay about it along with their grandparents' names and addresses. Gambrell then wrote to the grandparents, asking if he could borrow the object to exhibit in the Hall of State during the Centennial Exposition. When the Exposition closed, he wrote them a second letter asking if they wanted the object back. If that letter went unanswered, the artifact went into the Dallas Historical Society collection. The legal title to most of the collection was probably clouded by Gambrell's system, but no one ever showed up to claim anything.

The collection included about five hundred branding irons that had been exhibited at the Centennial. These had not been part of Gambrell's Hall of State exhibit but had been collected by Gus Ford, a historian attached to the Live Stock Division of the Exposition. Texans have always been a little nutty about cattle brands, regarding them not as mere marks of ownership on cattle but as prairie equivalents of the coats of arms displayed by English aristocrats. In fact, eastern writers have described them as "the heraldry of the plains," and in the West the phrase "riding for the brand" has become a synonym for loyalty. No matter what symbolic value they carry, an exhibit of five hundred branding irons can be a little boring. Ford, however, took a leaf from Gambrell's approach. He asked the donor of each iron to write a short history of the brand, and then he published the brand designs and the histories in a book called *Texas Cattle Brands: A Catalog of the Texas Centennial Exposition Exhibit.* It is one of my favorite Texas books.

Ford wrote a preface in which he distinguishes four stages in the evolution of Texas cattle brands, an analysis I have never encountered anywhere else. First, he says, came the Spanish-Mexican brands, which are usually single letters embellished with hooks and curlicues, possibly derived from the rubrics with which eighteenth-century Spanish gentlemen signed their names. These were followed by pre-Civil War Anglo-American brands, usually simple monograms or initials placed on the animals' necks or jaws. The open-range ranching that developed after the Civil War required brands that could be read at a distance and could not be easily altered by thieves, and this led to what Ford calls "signboard brands," last names like Dyer, Young, and Grome spelled out on an animal's side, or brands like the Long Rail, a brand that, he says, "began at the steer's neck and ran backwards until there was no hair to burn." These were applied with a running iron, a straight bar or a ring heated in the fire and used like a pencil. The final stage began in the 1880s and represented a return to smaller brands that often incorporated symbols as well as letters and were placed low on an animal's hip with a stamp iron. Ford attributes this change to two causes: the development of fenced pastures, which eliminated the need for long-distance brand reading, and the demand by leather manufacturers for unblemished cow hides.

The best part of Ford's book is the illustrations of the brands and the accompanying narratives about them sent in by their owners. The Bar MD, as B. M. Halbert of Sonora wrote, was started by his uncle, J. C. Barksdale, and was read "Bar Money Down," because as a young man Barksdale had sold some heifers to a friend on credit and was never paid for them. From then on, he swore, any sales were going to be cash money down. Meyer Halff's brand, two interlocking half circles, registered in Pecos County in 1898, was called the Quien Sabe (Who Knows), because that was the answer one of Halff's cowboys gave when asked how to read it. According to F. G. Alexander of Haskell, another brand, the Flying Half Circle Diamond and a Half, was known in Haskell County as the Fleur de Mustard because when it first appeared on that range a group of cowboys argued about how to read it and one of them said, "It must be the Fleur de Mustard." "We just let it stand at that," Alexander, who was one of the cowboys, wrote. There was, in fact, a Fleur de Lis brand registered in Tom Green County, where it was known as the Flowering Lucy. Another Tom Green County brand, registered by W. M. Allen in 1880, is an open A followed by two open sixes. I would read it as A Sixty Six, but J. O. Allen of Strawn said it was always known as the A Hookety Hook.

One mysterious brand is from right here in Jeff Davis County and was sent to the Centennial by A. G. Prude. It is an open square hat with a T superimposed on it, registered in Jeff Davis County by Looney and Prude in 1885. According to Prude, it was known as the Grab All or The Hell. There has to be a story behind that.

May 17, 2012

✣ 41 ✣

MADELINE IN TEXAS

Ludwig Bemelmans and John Bemelmans Marciano,
Madeline in Texas.
New York: Arthur A. Levine, 1999.

"IN AN OLD HOUSE in Paris that was covered with vines / Lived twelve little girls in two straight lines." This was the opening couplet of Ludwig Bemelmans's classic children's book *Madeline,* first published in 1939, and the rhyme was repeated at the beginning of each of the five *Madeline* books that followed it. The books are about the adventures of a little girl who lives in a convent school in Paris with eleven other little girls, a dog named Genevieve, and their teacher, Miss Clavel. Madeline is precocious, curious, loyal to her friends, and everything a little girl should be, and the books, which eventually included *Madeline's Rescue, Madeline and the Bad Hat, Madeline and the Gypsies, Madeline in London,* and *Madeline's Christmas,* have been beloved by several generations of parents and children. Most of those readers do not know that there is a seventh Madeline book set in Texas.

I first discovered Bemelmans when I was a teenager through a series of whimsically illustrated travel articles he wrote for *Holiday* magazine and his 1946 book *Hotel Bemelmans,* a slightly fictionalized and hilarious account of his years as a hotel employee in New York. I loved Bemelmans's pieces because he was my ideal of a cosmopolitan sophisticate, a bon vivant, artist, and man of the world, just the kind of person I wanted to be when I grew up.

Bemelmans was born in 1898 into a family of hotel owners in the Austrian Tyrol. As a youth he was apprenticed with disastrous results to hotels all over Austria and finally given a choice of being sent to reform school or emigrating to America. He arrived in New York in 1914 at the age of sixteen and got a job as a busboy at the Ritz-Carlton, where he eventually became assistant manager of the banquet department, a position that enabled him to buy a used Hispano-Suiza automobile, hire a chauffeur, take art lessons, and enjoy the Bohemian society of 1920s New York.

In the 1930s Bemelmans quit his hotel job and, on the strength of his art lessons, started drawing a comic strip for a children's magazine. He sold cartoons to the *Saturday Evening Post* and illustrations to advertising agencies, and illustrated a children's book by Monroe Leaf, the author of the immensely popular *Story of Ferdinand*. He married, had a daughter, and took his family to visit Paris, where he conceived the idea for the first *Madeline* book, *Madeline*. In the 1940s and 50s he became a well-known and prolific author and illustrator, writing not only the other *Madeline* books but several novels and numerous articles for *Town and Country*, *Holiday*, and the *Ladies Home Journal*, and doing covers for the *New Yorker* and other magazines. He and his wife, Mimi, traveled extensively and made many friends.

One of those friends was Stanley Marcus, who described Bemelmans as "the single most charming spirit I've ever run into." It was Bemelmans's friendship with Marcus that produced the seventh *Madeline* book, *Madeline in Texas*. As Jeannie Ralston recounted in her review in the October 1999 issue of *Texas Monthly*, Bemelmans and his wife came to Texas in 1955 to write a travel article. While they were here they stopped in Dallas to spend a few days with the Marcuses. The Marcuses gave them a tour of Dallas and took them to the Fort Worth Stock Show, where Bemelmans oversampled a dish that was new to him—corny dogs—and a doctor had to be called. Before they left Dallas

Marcus persuaded Bemelmans to write a Christmas story for Neiman Marcus to use in its upcoming Christmas promotion (Bemelmans had done the cover for Neiman's Christmas catalogue a few years before). The result was a rhyming tale called "Madeline's Christmas in Texas." The story was serialized in a series of Neiman Marcus ads in the Dallas and Houston papers, accompanied by pen and ink sketches by Bemelmans. There is a rumor that the text and sketches were bound into a small book that was given away to Neiman's customers, but I have never seen a copy.

The burden of Bemelmans's Texas story is that two days before Christmas, Madeline's Texan great-grandfather dies and leaves her his fortune, which includes a ranch, a gold mine, an oil field, and his shares in Neiman Marcus. Madeline, her eleven classmates, her dog, and Miss Clavel all fly to Texas to inspect her inheritance. They are met by her great-grandfather's lawyer, who greets them at the airport with "Merry Christmas and howdy, ma'am / The name is Crockett, but call me Sam." Lawyer Crockett, after providing all of the little girls with boots and Stetsons, takes them on a tour of Madeline's property, including the oil field ("Yippiyay! We're just in time to usher / In a million barrel gusher"). The tour ends with a visit to Neiman's, where Madeline manages to get separated from the other girls and is locked in when the store closes. She is rescued by a dauntless Texas Ranger called by Miss Clavel ("In Texas when anyone's in danger / You call upon the TEXAS RANGER") and everything ends happily on Christmas morning when the little girls' and Miss Clavel's hotel room is filled with presents from Neiman's.

The little story might have been completely forgotten, but thirty years after Bemelmans death in 1962, his grandson, John Bemelmans Marciano, was working on a biography of his grandfather and found the manuscript and drawings for *Madeline's Christmas in Texas*. Marciano had been teaching himself to draw in his grandfather's style and he provided new illustrations for the text and published it as part of a larger edition of his grandfather's writings under the title *Madeline in America and Other Holiday Tales* (Arthur A. Levine, 1999). With Stanley Marcus's help, the publisher brought out an abbreviated edition containing only the text of the original 1955 story and Marciano's illustrations under the title *Madeline in Texas* and so, thirty-seven years after Bemelmans's death, another *Madeline* book was added to the canon.

To mark its publication, Marcus donated a share of Neiman Marcus stock to Dallas's Hockaday School for Girls, with the provision that the dividends would be used to fund a Madeline Scholarship for study in the US, France, or England "as a constant reminder of Madeline and her curiosity."

September 10, 2015

42

LONE STAR LAWMEN

Robert M. Utley, *Lone Star Lawmen: The Second Century of the Texas Rangers.*
New York: Oxford University Press, 2007.

IT SEEMS as though a new Texas Ranger book comes out every other year or so. Two years ago it was Joaquin Jackson's *One Ranger*; this year it is Robert M. Utley's *Lone Star Lawmen: The Second Century of the Texas Rangers*, published by Oxford University Press. They are very different books. Jackson's is the most recent in a long series of memoirs by former Rangers, a tradition stretching all the way back to 1848, when Ranger Samuel Reid published his *Scouting Expedition of McCullough's Texas Rangers*. These books recount their authors' experiences as Rangers over a short span of years, and sometimes reveal their egos, but most of them provide few dispassionate insights into the Rangers as an institution or offer any judgments concerning their efficacy as a law-enforcement agency. Utley's book belongs to a much shorter tradition, histories of the Rangers written by professional historians, and it provides both insights and judgments and tells some good stories in the process. As the subtitle indicates, it is the second and final volume in Utley's history of the Rangers from 1844 to the present. The first volume, *Lone Star Justice: The First Century of the Texas Rangers*, was published by Oxford in 2002.

Utley is well-qualified to write such a history. He is one of the leading Western historians in the United States, a retired chief historian of the National Park Service, and the author of a list of books about the West as long as your arm, including a biography of Custer and a two-volume history of the Indian Wars. Not only that, he is well-acquainted with Texas and especially the Big Bend, and he should have a special place in the hearts of everyone who lives in Fort Davis. Utley was the National Park Service employee who came to inspect the ruins of the old military post at Fort Davis in 1960 when the Park Service was debating whether or not to acquire them. He wrote a report that was so favorable that it tipped the balance toward acquisition, and the next year the old fort became a National Historic Site. Not only that, Park Service insiders have told me that it was Utley's report that led to the decision to restore key buildings at the fort rather than stabilize them as ruins. Utley returned to Fort Davis several times in the early 1960s to do research on the fort, and he has fond memories of the town.

There are three reasons that Utley's book is so good. He makes full use of the Adjutant General's Records and the Department of Public Safety Records, which are the ultimate sources for Texas Ranger history (sadly, a large chunk of the Ranger records at the Department of Public Safety are missing, either through carelessness or deliberate destruction). He writes like a dream. And he views the past with the dispassionate eye of a trained historian and pulls no punches. Walter Prescott Webb, who was also a professional historian, wrote the last history of the Rangers in 1935. But Webb was a romantic who admired the Rangers, knew them and traveled with them and could not bring himself to speak ill of their deeds. Utley presents a much more balanced view. He excoriates the vicious Captain Harry Lee Ransom, who during the so-called "bandit war" in the Lower Rio Grande Valley in 1915 bragged of "evaporating" suspicious Mexicans (a few years later the Soviets employed a similar euphemism, "liquidate," for the same thing) but at the same time he praises Rangers like Manuel T. Gonzuallas and Frank Hamer for their cool courage and their investigative skills. He does, however, acknowledge their flamboyant egotism, which with Gonzuallas took the form of driving an armor-plated 1932 Chrysler with a machine gun mounted on the dashboard, and with Hamer manifested itself in his claim to have been the sole architect of the strategy that nailed Bonnie Parker and Clyde Barrow, when their ambush was actually engineered by a Louisiana sheriff. Egotism seems to have been issued with Ranger badges in the 20s and 30s; even the relatively modest William Sterling sported a Western shirt with the words "General Bill" embroidered over one pocket when he served as Adjutant General.

Utley's main thesis is that the Rangers in the years between 1900 and 1935 were a very different bunch of folks from the post-1935 Rangers. The watershed came when the legislature made the Rangers one unit of a newly created Department of Public Safety, and they became a highly professional and specialized crime-detection force, well-paid and removed from political influence. The earlier Rangers, Utley points out, were tough men who had to deal with tough, lawless times—oil boom towns, bootleggers, border raiders, and race riots—and their six-shooter mentality was usually, with a few glaring exceptions such as Captain Ransom, appropriate to those times. The largest flaw in the Ranger organization in those years was that every Ranger, from senior captain down to private, served at the pleasure of the governor and thus had to endure a political test every two years. In the 1918 election Governor William Hobby used the Rangers, including the notorious Captain Hansen at Marfa, to assess the strength of his opponent's supporters. When Miriam Ferguson took office for the second time in 1933, she fired the entire Ranger force of forty-four men and replaced them with political appointees. In addition, she appointed 2,344 special Rangers, all of whom had police authority and could carry pistols. As Utley says, "Every night club and gambling house had its special ranger guard." It was these abuses that finally led to the reorganization of the Rangers under the leadership of Department of Public Safety director Homer Garrison in 1935 and to their emergence as an elite crime-detecting and crime-fighting force.

In the 1960s, due to some first-hand experience in a Rio Grande Valley farm workers' strike, I was among those who were convinced that the Texas Rangers were an anachronism and should be abolished. Utley's book has convinced me that today they are a force of which all Texans can be proud.

September 20, 2007

✣ 43 ✣

THE BIG RICH

Bryan Burrough, *The Big Rich: The Rise and Fall of the Greatest Texas Oil Fortunes.* New York: Penguin Press, 2009.

Bryan Burrough's *The Big Rich* is essentially a group biography of four Texas oilmen, Sid Richardson, Clint Murchison, Roy Cullen, and H. L. Hunt, and their families (Hunt had three of them simultaneously). All four men started out as wildcatters in the 1920s and became immensely wealthy by the 1940s. Burrough gets all of the legends of the Texas oil fields into the book and documents most of them. He tells how Sid Richardson, down on his luck in the 1930s and unable to pay his office rent, operated from a counter stool and phone booth in a Fort Worth drug store; if he was out of the store trying to hustle a deal, the soda jerk would answer the pay phone for him, saying, "Mr. Richardson's office." When his wells finally started coming in Richardson bought the drug store and gave it to the soda jerk. Burrough tells how H. L. Hunt once talked Dad Joiner out of an entire East Texas oil field, then persuaded Joiner not to file suit against him when the field started producing beyond all expectation. Everything you ever heard about the Texas oil business is in this book, with footnotes.

Burrough pays considerable attention to the role that wealthy oilmen played in creating an image of Texas as a place of unlimited and uninhibited wealth, and of Texans as loud-talking, big-spending boors in the Silver Dollar Jim West mold. He picks 1948 as a key year in the creation of that image, pointing out that in 1948 *Life*, *Fortune*, and *Time* all carried elaborate feature stories on Texas oilmen and their eccentricities, and that a spate of books and movies about Texas oilmen followed, including Edna Ferber's *Giant* and John Bainbridge's *The Superamericans*.

Here is where I have to disagree with Burrough. I think the image of loud-talking, free-spending Texas millionaires goes way back before 1948 and even before the discovery of oil in Texas. Edna Ferber's Jett Rink, the oilman in *Giant*, was based on Houston oilman Glenn McCarthy, but long before McCarthy and Hunt, Richardson, Murchison, and Cullen, there was Shanghai Pierce. Pierce was the original prototype for the loud, rich, Texan, and he was both loud and rich. He came to Texas from Rhode Island at the age of nineteen in 1853 with seventy-five cents in his pocket, and, when he died in 1900, he owned two hundred thousand acres of land, and his estate was valued at $1,320,000. He was endowed with a voice that could be heard a block away in normal conversation. There was a story that he built the bunkhouse on his Wharton County ranch three hundred yards from his residence so that his cowboys could not hear him whispering to his wife. He stood six feet four in his stocking feet, and he was both crude and flamboyant. He was given to walking into clubrooms in Kansas City and introducing himself as "Shanghai Pierce, Webster on cattle, by God." He laid out a town adjacent to his ranch headquarters west of Wharton which included a hotel and a church. When a visitor asked him if he belonged to the church, he replied, "Hell, no. That church belongs to me." He was called "Shanghai" because when he was a young man someone said that he strutted like a Shanghai rooster, and the name stuck. Before he died, he had a marble statue of himself erected in a pasture on his ranch, and he is buried under it.

When Pierce appeared on the national stage, it had already been set by Eastern journalists who had been telling the public about the crudities of Texas cowboys for fifteen years. On the wall of my study is a woodcut illustration from *The National Police Gazette* with the title, "An Unpleasant Guest." It depicts a cowboy with a Bowie knife between his teeth, waving a pistol in each hand, in the center of an opulent ballroom. Men in evening dress and ladies in gowns and jewels are shrinking away from him. The text accompanying the illustration says that it portrays a scene that occurred in a Leadville, Colorado, hotel when a Texas cowboy decided to liven up a formal ball. This illustration is just one of hundreds that appeared in the tabloid press and even in sedate magazines like *Harper's* between 1870 and 1885, along with stories detailing the outrageous behavior of Texas cowboys in civilized society. When journalists encountered Pierce on his trips to Kansas City in the 1880s, he fit right into the mold they had created for Texas cowboys, and he was rich besides. "I am a pretty big dog in the puddle," he was fond of saying. He enjoyed playing the country bumpkin. After taking his wife and daughter to Europe, he told his friends in San Antonio that he'd gone to Rome to see the Papal Bulls, but all he could find were some scrawny cows outside of town.

Although Pierce could country-boy when it suited him, he was a calculating businessman at bottom, and he bragged about that, too. After besting San Antonio banker Daniel Sullivan in a business deal, he got on a train and told a passenger coach full of listeners, "I think it is the best commercial record a man can make if he can prove in court that he robbed little Dannie Sullivan. I'll be very popular for this. The people will descend upon me and pluck my locks for souvenirs and charms." No one in that coach ever forgot Shanghai Pierce.

Pierce acquired a national audience when he became the model for Maverick Brander, the leading character in Charles Hoyt's 1890 Broadway hit, *A Texas Steer.* Brander, a rich rancher from Red Dog, Texas, gets elected to Congress and astounds

Washington society with his antics. The play was so popular that it was made into a movie in 1915, with Tyrone Power Sr. playing Brander, and again in 1927, with Will Rogers in the role of the rancher-congressman. According to Pierce's obituaries, Hoyt had met Pierce in the 1880s and was fascinated by him. Pierce also inspired the leading character in an enormously popular novel by Archibald Clavering Gunter, *Mr. Potter of Texas*, published in 1888 and turned into a five-act play in 1891. Pierce was reading Gunter's novel the night he died in 1900. By that time, everyone in America knew that Texas was full of millionaire braggarts. We are still trying to live Shanghai Pierce's legacy down.

October 21, 2009

44

NORFLEET

J. Frank Norfleet, *Norfleet.*
Fort Worth: White Publishing Co., 1924.

On a recent trip to the Panhandle I drove through Hale Center, a small town on Interstate 27 between Lubbock and Canyon whose most famous resident was J. Frank Norfleet. In the 1930s there were three famous J. Franks in Texas: J. Frank Dobie, J. Frank Norris, and J. Frank Norfleet. J. Frank Dobie, of course, was a professor of English at the University of Texas, a newspaper columnist, the author of numerous books on Texas folklore, and "Mr. Texas" to the nation. J. Frank Norris was the fundamentalist pastor of the First Baptist Church in Fort Worth and probably the most controversial Baptist preacher in America, a distinction not easy to achieve in a denomination noted for controversy. J. Frank Norfleet was for a few years the nation's best-known amateur detective.

Norfleet was an unlikely detective. For the first half of his life he was a West Texas cowboy and rancher. His cowboy skills, which he first demonstrated in the 1880s as a hand on the Snyder Brothers ranch near Muleshoe, won him a job as foreman of the 262,000-acre Spade Ranch in Lamb and Hockley Counties. Norfleet managed the Spade until 1906, when he and his wife settled down to raise horses on their own small place near Hale Center, and that is what he was doing when he went to Dallas in

November 1919 to see Captain Dick Slaughter about buying some land from him.

Norfleet must have stood out in downtown Dallas as the country boy that he was because he immediately fell into the hands of a gang of confidence men. One of them, posing as a mule buyer from Hillsboro, Texas, engaged him in a conversation in the lobby of his hotel, and together they discovered a wallet stuffed with money in the cushions of the sofa they were sitting on. The owner's name was in it, J. B. Stetson (they were not very inventive confidence men), and of course he turned out to be a guest in the hotel. Norfleet went up to his room to return the wallet and was offered a $100 reward, which he refused. Stetson told Norfleet that he was a member of the New York Stock Exchange and offered to invest the $100 for Norfleet, which Norfleet agreed to. The next day Stetson told Norfleet that his investment had earned $800, which he handed over to him along with a proposition for further investments. Over a few more days of complicated negotiations involving several of Stetson's associates, Norfleet turned $45,000 of his own money and $90,000 in borrowed funds over to the alleged stockbrokers, who then skipped town.

At that point, he wrote later, he said to himself, "Forty-five thousand dollars gone! Ninety thousand dollars in debt! Fifty-four years old! What was I to do?" Norfleet did what any good cowboy would do. He took the bull by the horns. He went back to Hale Center, got himself deputized by the sheriff there, and took off after the gang that had victimized him. He followed them from city to city across the United States and into Canada and Mexico and Cuba. He discovered that they were part of a larger ring of bunco artists that were bilking unwary ranchers and farmers by setting up fake "stock exchanges" in hotel rooms all over the Midwest, and he eventually brought the four men who had swindled him and seventy-five of their associates to justice.

J. FRANK NORFLEET

Newspapers and magazines all over the country carried stories about his exploits, and in 1924 he published a book, simply entitled *Norfleet*, recounting his adventures. Throughout the 1920s he received hundreds of letters from people asking for his services as a private detective. *Norfleet* went through several printings and at least three editions. In the 1950s, when I first started accumulating Texas books, you could find a copy or two in any used bookstore in Texas. Its sales helped Norfleet recoup his losses, and it remains the only full-length book by an American confidence game victim. Norfleet himself lived to the ripe age of 103 and is buried in the Hale Center cemetery. The next time I am up that way I intend to stop and pay homage to a remarkable Texan.

September 22, 2005

✣ 45 ✣

THE AMAZING TALE OF MR. HERBERT AND HIS FABULOUS ALPINE COWBOYS BASEBALL CLUB

DJ Stout, *The Amazing Tale of Mr. Herbert and His Fabulous Alpine Cowboys Baseball Club: An Illustrated History.* Austin: University of Texas Press, 2010.

SEVERAL SATURDAYS ago I went over to Alpine to spend the day at the Way Out West Texas Book Festival. This is an annual event put on by the Alpine Rotary Club, now in its third year and getting better every year. For me the high point of this year's program was hearing DJ Stout talk about his new book on the Alpine Cowboys baseball team, *The Amazing Tale of Mr. Herbert and His Fabulous Alpine Cowboys Baseball Club*, just released by the University of Texas Press.

Stout, an Austin graphic designer who eschews periods after his initials, intended to give a power point presentation of photos from his book, but the power point projector didn't work (do they ever?), so instead he picked up a mike and talked for forty-five minutes *ex tempore* about his father, his mother, the family dog, the Marine Corps, Herbert Kokernot, the Cowboys ball club, Dan Blocker, and half a dozen other subjects. His talk hung together because Stout's book is a tribute to his retired Marine officer father, Doyle Stout, whom Herbert Kokernot Jr. recruited out of high school to pitch for the Alpine Cowboys. It is also a tribute to

Herbert Kokernot Jr., the Alpine rancher who loved baseball so much that he built a stadium and organized his own team just for the pleasure of watching them play—and win. And it is clearly a labor of love, a book that grew out of Stout's childhood fascination with his father's old team.

In his talk Stout told how his father, the son of a Dallas Pentecostal preacher, started playing baseball for a Salvation Army team when he was twelve and developed into a spectacular left-handed pitcher at Dallas's Crozier Technical High School. He had no thought of going to college, but Herbert Kokernot saw him play in the 1952 state high school championship tournament and invited him to come to Alpine and play for the Cowboys, offering to pay his tuition and expenses at Sul Ross to boot.

Stout said his father met his mother, the daughter of a Van Horn rancher, at a Sul Ross dance, and Stout himself was born at the old Alpine hospital which was, as he put it, just a long home run from the center field fence of Kokernot Field. He is definitely an Alpine boy. A lot of his talk that morning was about the generosity of Herbert Kokernot, who not only provided his players with first-class uniforms and equipment but paid their living expenses, took them and their wives on vacation trips, and handed out bonuses for home runs and strikeouts.

Kokernot's generosity was not limited to his own team. Stout told how in 1948 Kokernot took his Cowboys to the National Semipro Baseball Tournament in Wichita, Kansas, and put them up in air-conditioned comfort at the best hotel in town. The Cowboys were knocked out of the tournament after losing their first two games, but in the meantime Kokernot had befriended the manager of an underdog team from Glenridge, New Jersey, called the Tydols. The Tydols unexpectedly won their first game, but their manager confessed to Kokernot that the team did not have enough money to stay in Wichita if they advanced further through the playoffs, even though they were sleeping on cots in a warehouse. Kokernot not only offered to pay all of their expenses for as long as they were in the tournament, he moved them into the Cowboy's vacated hotel rooms. The Tydols played their remaining games calling themselves the New Jersey Kokernots. They ended up in fourth place. Kokernot, fearing that his own Cowboys might think he had abandoned them, took all of his players and their wives to Colorado Springs for a vacation before returning to Alpine.

The best story that Stout told was about the time that Kokernot recruited three Eastern college boys for the Cowboys. He told them to take the train to Marathon, where they would be met by a car. They got off the train at Marathon and started for Alpine in a car driven by Bob Bilgrave, a regular Cowboys player. The Easterners had never been in the West before, and they were staring out of the car windows at the desert scenery when they came over a hill and found three cowboys standing in the middle of the road, bandanas pulled over their faces, and drawn pistols pointed at the car. Bilgrave stopped the car and the biggest cowboy, a huge man, walked to the back door, yanked it open, and pulled the three Easterners out into the road, ordering them to hand over their wallets and watches. When the bandits had collected their loot they climbed the fence, jumped on the horses they had tied there, and galloped off.

The three Easterners were white and shaken. Bilgrave told them that the best thing to do was to drive on to Alpine and go to the lobby of the Holland Hotel, where the sheriff could usually be found, and ask him to raise a posse to pursue the bandits. When they got to the Holland, Gene Hendrix, the owner of the Alpine radio station, happened to be there, and when he heard their story he said, "Let's go to the radio station and put it on the air. That's the quickest way to get a posse." When they got to the station Hendrix gave one of the Eastern boys the mike, and he was telling his story when the front door flew open and the three gunmen burst in, pistols drawn. The Easterners threw up their hands; the gunmen pulled down their masks and shouted, "Welcome to Alpine!" The biggest cowboy was Dan Blocker, just beginning his acting career.

Herbert Kokernot's Cowboys played ball at Kokernot Field for fifteen seasons, from 1947 through 1961. Stout's book documents each season with beautiful black-and-white photographs by Alpine's Charles Hunter, the Cowboy's official photographer, with text by Stout, and with sidebars captioned "Cowboy Tales," reminiscences of surviving team members collected by Stout. These may be the best parts of the book.

Herbert Kokernot's grandson, Chris Lacy, introduced Stout's talk. That afternoon Lacy, his wife Dawn, and Stout all went out to Kokernot Field to see the resuscitated Big Bend Cowboys trample the Las Cruces Vaqueros 14-1 to win the Continental League Championship, a perfect ending to a great baseball day.

August 19, 2010

✣ 46 ✣

MARFA

Kathleen Shafer, *Marfa: The Transformation of a Texas Town.*
Austin: University of Texas Press, 2017.

IN 1955 Texas novelist Bill Brammer, writing about the filming of *Giant* for the *Texas Observer*, described Marfa as "this bleak and blissful and totally unworldly little town." Marfa may still be bleak to some and blissful to others, but it is no longer unworldly. Kathleen Shafer's new book, *Marfa: The Transformation of a West Texas Town*, explains why. Tim Johnson once told me that people come into his Marfa Book Company every day and ask if there is not a book that will help them understand Marfa. This may be it.

Shafer, a slender gray-eyed woman in her thirties, first came to Marfa in 2007 because of her interest in the history of airports. She was drawn here by the abandoned Marfa Army Airfield, and that is what we talked about when I first met her. But then she met the late Cecilia Thompson, and in the first chapter of her book she tells how Thompson, whom she describes as "a wickedly smart old lady," told her how Donald Judd's twenty-year presence in Marfa had transformed Marfa from a dying ranching town into an internationally famous art community and, more recently, into an international tourist destination. That is the transformation that Shafer explores in her book, which was originally written as a PhD dissertation in geography at the University of Texas in Austin and was published this year by the University of Texas Press. It is refreshingly free of academic jargon and full of surprises, even for someone like me who has been observing and writing about Marfa for fifteen years.

One of the surprises is the amount of scholarly literature already devoted to Marfa. In her footnotes Shafer cites a dissertation at Binghamton University, an honors thesis at Bates College, and articles in journals like *Applied Research in Economic Development* and *The Annals of Tourism Research*. Who knew?

Another surprise is the amount of detailed coverage Shafer is able to give to events in Marfa over the past twenty years, which she considers as a crucial period in Marfa's transformation. She treats in considerable depth the controversies surrounding the destruction of the hospital ruins at Fort D. A. Russell, the erection of the Playboy sculpture/advertisement on US 90, the routing of air force bomber training runs over the Big Bend, and the recent discussion of Airbnbs and the lack of low-cost housing in Marfa. Shafer writes, "I've read, watched, or listened to every piece of media focused on Marfa since 1983," and I believe it.

Marfa has actually undergone several transformations during its 134-year history. The Mexican Revolution brought a thriving and enterprising Hispanic population—refugees from the violence that swept Mexico between 1910 and 1920, and World War II and the development of the Army air base here caused the town's population to triple. Shafer acknowledges these transformations in her earlier chapters, saying that the factors that shaped Marfa's early history were ranching, its proximity to the border, and the presence of the military at Fort D. A. Russell. Her main focus, though, is on Judd and the aftermath of his residence here, and her strongest chapters are the one on Judd's career and his complicated relationship with the Dia Foundation and the people of Marfa, and the one on the post-Judd marketing or "branding" of Marfa, exemplified by the fact that Prada Marfa is not in Marfa but a few miles west of Valentine, thirty miles away. She cites the UK-based publication *Marfa Journal* and J. Crew's leather Marfa Bags (not made in Marfa) as examples. I was reminded of my friend C. M. Mayo, who is working on a guidebook to the Big Bend and has been releasing segments of the text as podcasts under the title "Marfa Mondays." When I asked her why she called them "Marfa Mondays" when most of the content is about other parts of the Big Bend, she said, "Everyone in New York knows where Marfa is, but no one there has ever heard of the Big Bend."

Shafer's style is refreshingly non-academic. She occasionally drops into the first person, and she sometimes admits she does not know things. My favorite footnote is the one to the sentence in Chapter 6 in which she suggests that the name of the British publication *Marfa Journal* is an example of Marfa marketing: "I'm taking a leap here," she writes, "because my request to *Marfa Journal* on the source of the name was not returned. So it could be a Russian source, but I doubt it."

In Chapter 3 Shafer shifts gears slightly and attempts to apply three concepts utilized by geographers—landscape, space, and place—to Marfa. In my opinion this is the least successful chapter in the book (which is another way of saying that I had considerable difficulty in understanding it), but paradoxically it yields Shafer's best insight. "Place in Marfa," she writes, "can be experienced in countless ways, based on the needs and desires of the inhabitant or visitor. It is experiential perspective, where the experience is the culmination of sensation, perception, and conception. What does the place of Marfa entail? It is the combination of the people who live here and those who are visiting. It is the quiet activity that occurs each weekday inside the library, or the sounds of the espresso machine inside Frama, where a two-person line constitutes a rush. It is the patio of Jett's Grill in the Hotel Paisano on an early evening, when it is cool enough to sit outside, and where you are more likely to know someone there than not." She could have added the bustle of Mando's at lunch or the sound of hoof beats at a Saturday afternoon calf-roping to her list. The point is that residents lead their own lives, whether they are artists or ranch hands, and tourists bring their own expectations, so there are as many Marfas as there are observers of Marfa. "It's up to you to define what the sense of place is for you," Shafer writes.

Marfa: The Transformation of a West Texas Town was reviewed favorably in the December 16 *Wall Street Journal* by William Spiegelman, who called it "a love letter to a community." This may be only an example of Shafer's assertion that the word Marfa will sell anything, but it is quite an achievement for a first-time author to receive a glowing review in the *WSJ*, so if you run into Shafer on the street in Marfa, congratulate her, and then go buy her book.

January 18, 2018

✣ 47 ✣

H. ALLEN SMITH, A NEW YORKER IN ALPINE

ONE OF America's best-known authors once lived in Alpine and wrote his last and best book there. H. Allen Smith was a humorist whose first three books sold nearly a million and a half copies during World War II. He went on to write thirty-seven more books and hundreds of magazine articles, but by 1967, when he moved to Alpine, he was fifty-nine, and the most productive part of his career was behind him.

Smith was really a phenomenon of the 1930s, a hobo newspaperman who hit it big in New York. He got his first newspaper job in Huntington, Indiana, when he was fifteen—he never finished high school—and worked for newspapers in five states before landing a job as a feature writer with United Press in New York in 1929. In 1934 he moved over to the *New York World-Telegram,* where he apparently modeled himself on Hildy Johnson, the hard-drinking, tough-talking reporter hero of *The Front Page*, the play written by Smith's friends Ben Hecht and Charles MacArthur. He became part of a circle of writers and night-club habitués that included Hecht and MacArthur as well as Damon Runyon, James Thurber, Walter Winchell, and Ring Lardner.

In 1941 Smith published *Low Man on a Totem Pole,* an account of the characters he had met as a New York newspaperman—entertainers, inventors, press agents, and just plain screwballs. It was an instant success. He quit his job at the *World-Telegram* and, as he put it, "never had to set an alarm clock again." *Life in a Putty Knife Factory* (1943) was more of the same, as was *Lost in the Horse Latitudes* (1944). The books kept Smith's name on the *New York Times* best-seller list for 108 weeks and made him the best-known humorous writer in America. They were particularly popular in their Armed Forces Editions; they appealed to servicemen's nostalgia for the glamour of prewar days.

It was chili that brought Smith to Alpine. In August 1967 Smith published an article in *Holiday* magazine entitled "Nobody Knows More About Chili Than I Do." When the article appeared, Frank Tolbert, Wick Fowler, and Carroll Shelby were organizing the first Terlingua Chili Cookoff, designed to promote Tolbert's book *A Bowl of Red* and sell land at Shelby's Terlingua Ranch Resort. The main contest was to be between Wick Fowler and Los Angeles restaurateur Dave Chasen, but at the last minute Chasen dropped out. Tolbert remembered Smith's article and invited him to take Chasen's place. The contest is another story, but Smith, who had been living in Mount Kisco, New York, fell in love with the Big Bend and decided to move to Alpine. He bought a lot on the hillside overlooking town and built a white brick ranch-style house with a red tile roof.

The love affair was short-lived. Smith was both irascible and profane in a casual New York way, and that did not go over well with his West Texas neighbors. He called people bastards and worse and was genuinely puzzled when they took offense. He fell out with the contractors who built his house over costs and over a brick tool shed that through some misunderstanding acquired an expensive picture window, and he complained loudly and publicly about them. He dropped names at parties and then was angered when he had to explain who the people whose names he had dropped were. It was not, as they say, a good fit.

The nadir of Smith's relationship with Alpine came in March

1970, when *Time* magazine's "People" section carried a paragraph quoting him as saying that the people of Alpine were "a bunch of bigoted, pious, lying, cheating, bastards." Never able to leave well enough alone, Smith then wrote an article for *True* magazine expounding on these sentiments and describing the local reaction to them, which included threats to tar and feather him. He told how an inebriated cowboy called him one night to give him what-for. Smith interrupted him with a double-barreled blast of profane invective. There was a shocked silence and then the cowboy said, "Why, you ain't nothing but an old popcorn poop." It was a perfectly calibrated response.

After the two articles were published, Smith received a surprisingly thick sheaf of congratulatory letters from Texans who had suffered from small-town prejudices themselves. Few of them were from Alpinians, but one Alpine resident who did like and admire Smith was Elton Miles, head of the English Department at Sul Ross. Miles realized that Smith's humor, with its meandering anecdotes and exaggerations, was squarely in the tradition of American frontier humor, and he described Smith as the greatest American humorist since Mark Twain. In 1972 Miles edited and wrote an introduction for a collection of Smith's magazine pieces, *The Best of H. Allen Smith*. Smith dedicated the book to Paul Forchheimer, another Alpine friend.

Smith published two somewhat convoluted comic novels set in Texas while living in Alpine, *The View from Chivo* and *The Return of the Virginian*. Smith's method of collecting material was to jot notes on overheard conversations, strange facts, and anything else that intrigued him on little slips of paper and stuff the slips in file drawers. The H. Allen Smith Papers at the Archives of the Big Bend are full of notes made in Alpine for these two books, usually just one or two sentences or even just a phrase heard in a café or on the street.

Smith missed his circle of New York friends, and in particular he missed his deceased boon companion Gene Fowler, legendary Denver journalist, Hollywood screenwriter, and biographer of John Barrymore. In Alpine he was able to relive his own newspaper days by writing a serious biography of Fowler. He worked on the book steadily the last two years of his life, and it was published posthumously by William Morrow after Smith's death from a heart attack on February 24, 1976. It is called *The Life and Legend of Gene Fowler*, and it might just be the best book ever written in the Big Bend. It is certainly H. Allen Smith's best book.

November 26, 2008

✣ 48 ✣

GROVER LEWIS, THE BEST WRITER NOBODY EVER HEARD OF

THE OTHER DAY my wife and I watched, courtesy of Netflix, Peter Bogdanovich's 1971 film, *The Last Picture Show*. The film is based on Larry McMurtry's novel with the same title, which was published in 1966, and which I happen to think is one of the best Texas novels ever written, if not the best. I saw the movie when it first came out and remembered being enormously impressed by it, both because of the deftness of Bogdanovich's direction and because virtually all the dialogue is taken directly from the novel, which is uncommon in movies made from books.

What I was not prepared for during this second viewing is that my old friend Grover Lewis appears on the screen for about thirty seconds, playing Sonny's father in the Christmas dance scene. I think I must have gone out for a bag of popcorn at that point the first time I saw the film, because it was a complete surprise to me. I knew Lewis in Fort Worth in the early 1960s, and he has been dead for thirteen years, but there he was on the screen, big as life and at his Grover-most.

I first met Grover in 1963, when we were both contributing book reviews to the *Fort Worth Star-Telegram*. I was paid $5 for each review (and I got to keep the book), but Grover was actually on the paper's payroll. He was several years older than I was, but he had lived about twice as long. In 1963 he had just been kicked out of a PhD program at Texas Tech for writing a scathing review in the school paper of an anti-Communist tract by the fundamentalist preacher Billy James Hargis and had been divorced by his wife. Behind that lay the most traumatic childhood I had ever heard of. When Grover was eight, his estranged parents had killed each other with the same pistol in a bizarre shoot-out in a San Antonio apartment; he had been sent to Fort Worth to live with his mother's sister and her husband, who constantly told him that he had "bad blood," and who were both, as Grover wrote years later, "abusive enough by today's standards to serve jail time." At thirteen he escaped to live in the Dallas suburb of Oak Cliff with a great-uncle, Spook Bailey, who had been a friend of Bonnie Parker and Clyde Barrow and who was the first adult who had treated him with any decency since his mother's death.

Grover lived on beer and pills in an apartment on Fort Worth's old South Side. He was nearly blind and wore coke-bottle-lens glasses, and his black hair stuck out in patches all over his head. He had sunken cheeks and a wide mouth and a ravaged face, and he habitually dressed in faded blue jeans and an old khaki Boy Scout shirt that had "Be Prepared" blazoned over one pocket, but he also had an old-fashioned Southern courtliness that contrasted with his alarming appearance. He stood up when a woman entered the room, had a beautiful smile, and believed in truth and justice. Robert E. Lee was one of his few heroes.

One winter day I showed up at the *Star-Telegram* office to hand in my book review at the same time as one of the other reviewers, a lovely young woman who was wearing a full-length, fur-trimmed coat that made her look like someone out of *Doctor Zhivago*. Grover joined us in the hallway, dressed in his jeans and Boy Scout shirt and with his morning beer in his hand. We went into the book editor's office and his secretary took one look at us and said, "My God, it's the whole book page at once."

Grover desperately wanted to write, and he started a novel, but he was totally unable to finish anything he started except book reviews and music criticism, and he had a hard time with those. He had the worst case of writer's block I have ever seen. He did turn out some laconic poems during those years, which were published in 1972 under the title *I'll Be There In the Morning if I Live.* In the late 1960s he moved to San Francisco and finally came into his own as a writer for the magazine *Rolling Stone*, where he produced a number of long pieces on film and music. For the next twenty years he contributed stories to *Rolling Stone, New West,* the *Washington Post,* and the *Los Angeles Times.* He developed an astringent, elegant, and ironic style that seemed to say that what he was writing about was all a joke but no one was allowed to laugh out loud. His friend Dave Hickey, another Fort Worth boy, once described him as "the most stone wonderful writer nobody ever heard of."

In 1992 Grover wrote a short piece for *Texas Monthly* about something he never discussed at any length with his friends: his parents' double murder and his childhood in Fort Worth and Oak Cliff. It was called "Farewell to Cracker Eden," and its favorable reception moved him to write more about his own troubled life, or, as he put it to Hickey, "to track the black beast to its lair." He submitted a proposal for a book to be called *Goodbye If You Call That Gone.* It was immediately accepted, and Grover started work on it. Shortly after he began writing, he was diagnosed with terminal lung cancer, and six weeks later he was dead.

Grover Lewis and Larry McMurtry were undergraduates together at North Texas State University, where they published a literary magazine called *The Coexistence Review.* McMurtry went on to publish a string of novels longer than your arm, and is still turning them out. Besides his book of poems, Grover saw one book of his prose published during his lifetime, a selection of his *Rolling Stone* articles on film production called *Academy All the Way,* published by Straight Arrow Press in San Francisco in 1974. Several years after his death Texas Monthly Press published a collection of his articles under the title *Splendor in the Short Grass.*

Larry McMurtry wrote the screenplay for Bogdanovich's *Last Picture Show*, and I am sure that it was Grover's friendship with McMurtry that opened the way for his appearance in the film. My memories of Grover had faded over the years, and I am grateful to McMurtry and Bogdanovich for bringing them so sharply back into focus.

October 23, 2008

✣ 49 ✣

ALAN TENNANT AND RATTLESNAKES

There are no rattlesnakes in England, so when the first English colonists came to North America rattlers made a big impression on them. One of the oldest American ballads is a song called "Springfield Mountain," written in the 1760s about a young man who is fatally bitten by a rattlesnake while mowing a meadow. He staggers to his beloved's house, and she tries to suck the poison out, but it enters a rotten tooth and they both die. The song ends, "Come all you friends, and warning take / Don't never get bit by a rattler snake."

The other day my neighbor, Alan Tennant, and I were discussing rattler snakes over lunch at Nel's in Fort Davis. While Tennant did not exactly write the book on rattlesnakes—that was done in 1956 by Laurence Monroe Klauber, whose 1,533-page *Rattlesnakes: Their Habits, Life Histories, and Influences on Mankind* is the last word on the subject—Tennant's book *Snakes of Texas*, published in 1984, covers the subject of Texas rattlers pretty thoroughly. There is a good story behind the publication of this book, but Tennant made me promise not to include it in this column because he's saving it for the book he plans to write himself someday.

There is a good story behind most of the events in Tennant's life, and a conversation with him tends to veer from tale to tale, a little like playing a very fast pinball machine. Tennant is a spring-loaded, wiry, athletic man in his late sixties with green eyes and a clipped black moustache that seems to grow upward from his lip. Over the years he has followed a falcon in an airplane from Texas to the Arctic, led birding tours to Africa, swum with sharks in the Gulf of Thailand, and pedaled a bicycle into the Colombian Andes. When I talked with him he had just returned from several weeks of trekking along the border between Myanmar and Thailand, hobnobbing with exiles from Myanmar on the Thai side of the line.

Our conversation about rattlesnakes was provoked by a recent newspaper photograph of a man holding a huge rattler killed near Coleman, Texas. Tennant explained the ways that the size of a dead rattlesnake can be inflated. The simplest, he said, was to hold the body of the snake up close to the camera lens while positioning yourself as far away from the lens as possible, which distorts the size of the snake in relation to your own body. Fishermen learned to do this shortly after cameras were invented. The outsized rattler skins mounted on boards in West Texas bars, he said, were created by wetting and slowly stretching the skin of a normal-sized snake. This technique can be easily detected because it leaves spaces between the scales, which would normally overlap. A less time-consuming way of achieving the same effect is to graft a rattlesnake head and tail onto a python skin, producing the kind of giant reptile that Tennant once saw displayed in a bar in Freer.

We discussed the number of stories about rattlesnakes that we had both heard growing up in Texas, and Tennant reminded me that the ultimate compendium of these stories was J. Frank Dobie's book *Rattlesnakes*, published posthumously in 1965, a year after Dobie's death. Dobie put every story he had ever heard about rattlesnakes into this volume, without vouching for the truth of any of them—he was a folklorist and not a scientist. He tells about rattlers killed that were eight feet long, ten feet long, even eighteen feet long. After recounting these whoppers he says,

"The way to make a record at snake-killing is to be off away from tape measures or yardsticks or scales and not to have too many witnesses."

Tennant assured me that the biggest rattlesnakes found in the wild in Texas ran about seven feet long. These are in the brush country of the lower Rio Grande Valley, where there is no winter and a snake can eat all year long, achieving a life span of ten to fifteen years. Snakes in captivity can eat more, live longer, and grow larger, Tennant said, adding with a shudder that in some of the less reputable roadside snake farms the reptiles are force-fed to increase their size.

We talked about stories concerning the power of the rattler's venom. Tennant said that one of the oldest and most frequently repeated of these is what he called the "Grandfather's Boot" story. It goes like this: Grandpa is bitten by a rattler out in a field and dies. He is wearing a fine pair of boots at the time, which his widow puts away in a closet after the funeral. Years later his grandson finds the boots and pulls them on, stands up, and keels over dead, because the fang of the rattler that killed Grandpa is still stuck in the boot and penetrates the boy's heel. Dobie tells an elaborate version of this story, involving a young cowboy who buys a fine pair of handmade boots to court his girl in. He is bitten by a rattler while wearing the boots and dies, leaving the boots to his best friend. The best friend falls in love with the dead man's girl, wears the boots to go courting, and he sickens and dies, leaving the boots to a third cowboy who courts the girl and wears the boots with the same result. The girl is suspected of having some fatal influence until a rattlesnake fang is found in one of the boots. Tennant says that these stories are absolute nonsense because the venom loses its efficacy after only a few hours' exposure to the atmosphere, and the fang is not poisonous in itself but is only a hollow tube that conducts the venom. Another rattlesnake story that can be dismissed, Tennant says, is that rattlesnakes can be deterred from sharing your bedroll at night by placing a horsehair rope around it before turning in. "Why would a critter that lives in a prickly pear patch be stopped by little old hairy rope?" he asked.

We agreed that one piece of folk advice found in the "Springfield Mountain" ballad was still good, and not just for lovers. One of the verses says, "And mind, when you're in love don't pass / Too near to patches of high grass." That's where the rattlers are.

November 24, 2010

50

JOHN W. THOMASON JR.: ARTIST, WRITER, AND MARINE

MY POST-ELECTION reading has been John W. Thomason Jr.'s *The Adventures of General Marbot*, published by Charles Scribner's Sons in 1935. Thomason, a Texan and a professional Marine officer, edited this five-hundred-page memoir of the Napoleonic Wars by a French general and illustrated it profusely with his inimitable pen-and-ink sketches. The book has taken me to another time and place, which has been a very good thing.

A copy of this book was in my parents' library, and I first read it when I was seven years old. It was the first adult book I ever read. I have remembered some of Marbot's descriptions and Thomason's drawings accompanying them ever since, for instance his account of how a military doctor cut a gangrene infection from his heel without any anesthetic and then poured a daily tot of brandy into the wound to disinfect it. I have enjoyed rereading it.

John W. Thomason Jr. was a Texas writer who has passed out of fashion but who I think is due for a second look. He was born in Huntsville in 1893, and he grew up in a genteel household full of books—he once told a friend that he had completed all of his serious reading by the time he was fifteen. From a very early age he loved to sketch birds and wildlife. He was uncertain about a career as a young man, but in April 1917, when the United States entered World War I, he joined the Marines and remained a Marine officer the rest of his life. In addition to being a professional Marine officer, he was also a professional artist and a professional writer, and his output was prodigious.

He went to France in 1918 as a platoon leader in the Fifth Marines and saw action at Belleau Wood, St. Mihiel, and in the Meuse-Argonne campaign. He was in his element, sketching whenever he could snatch a moment. A fellow Marine recalled him sitting on the edge of a foxhole, shells falling all around him, sketching with a burnt match on the back of a chocolate wrapper. When he came home after the war he was stationed at the Naval Ammunition Depot in Dover, New Jersey, and he exhibited some of his wartime sketches at Ackerman Galleries in New York. A fellow Marine, Lawrence Stallings, who later became famous as the author of *What Price Glory?*, persuaded him to take his portfolio to *Scribner's Magazine*, where Stallings had friends. The editor at *Scribner's* liked the sketches and asked Thomason if he could write some words to go with them for the magazine, and Thomason produced the six short stories about the Marines in France that Charles Scribner's Sons published in 1926 as Thomason's first book, *Fix Bayonets*.

Over the next eighteen years Thomason's military career took him and his wife, Leda, to Cuba, Nicaragua, and China, and to Stateside postings from Washington, DC, to California. He was a polished and elegant officer—his uniforms were tailor-made and he was very particular about their cut—and many of his postings had diplomatic overtones. He spent three years as a captain in the Marine Guard at the American Legation in Peking and two years as an aide to Assistant Secretary of the Navy Henry Roosevelt. He wrote and drew furiously during those years. In addition to his edition of Marbot's memoirs he contributed short stories to *Scribner's*, the *Saturday Evening Post*, the *New Yorker*, and the *American Mercury*, and he published three more volumes of short stories, a biography of Jeb Stuart, and two novels about early Texas, *Gone to Texas* in 1937 and *Lone Star Preacher*, which is acknowledged to be his masterpiece, in 1941. This is a novel about a Methodist preacher, Praxiteles Swan, who goes to the Civil War as a chaplain with Hood's Brigade. Thomason drew on an ex-Confederate chaplain he had known as a young man and on his grandfather's and great-uncles' memories of the war, and the result is the best Civil War book I know of by a Texan.

In the 1930s Thomason was regarded as a leading American writer. His annual income from royalties exceeded his service salary and allowances, and he counted Alexander Woollcott, Franklin P. Adams, and Will Rogers among his close friends. Ernest Hemingway thought that he was the best living American military writer, and included six Thomason pieces in his 1942 anthology *Men at War,* which Thomason helped him edit.

Thomason seems to have been the type of Southerner depicted by Caroline Gordon in her novel *Aleck Maury, Sportsman,* a quiet, reserved man, perhaps more comfortable with dogs and horses than people. His friend the explorer Roy Chapman Andrews, whom he hunted ducks with in Peking, wrote that "he had a warm smile and the soft voice, quiet dignity, and innate courtesy of a Southern gentleman." In one of the legends circulated among his fellow Marine officers, when a diplomat's wife in a South American capital asked him how he had enjoyed the three-day festivities accompanying a state visit, he replied, "Madam, I'd turn it all in on a good trottin' horse."

Thomason died while still in the service in 1944. He had desperately wanted to get into combat after Pearl Harbor and thought he had gotten his wish when he was assigned to Admiral Nimitz's staff in the Pacific in April 1943, but a combination of ulcers and double pneumonia invalided him back to the mainland, and he died in a Navy hospital in California in March 1944. He is buried in Huntsville, not far from Sam Houston's grave. Today his books are virtually unknown.

I have finished *The Adventures of General Marbot.* Marbot's hairbreadth escapes on the battlefields of Europe two hundred years ago took me far away from the opening week of the coming

Trump presidency, for which I am extremely grateful. They also pointed the way for a reading program for the next four years for me. I am going to spend those years reading Napoleonic War memoirs. There are hundreds of them. Every officer of field grade rank and above in the French and British armies spent their retirement years quarreling with each other in print, and the result is a vast sea of literature. Thomason mentions in a footnote in Marbot an eight-volume biography of the French Marshal Andre Massena. That ought to keep me occupied through at least the first year of the Trump administration.

December 1, 2016

✣ 51 ✣

WILLIAM HERVEY ALLEN ON THE MEXICAN BORDER

MY FRIEND Mike Cochran, who with his wife Linda Lavender resides in Denton and Fort Davis, Texas, and Montisi, Italy, is a collector of odds and ends and scraps of Texas history. He maintains a delightful website at mikecochran.net/history where you can learn, among other things, about Denton County's connection with Emperor Maximilian of Mexico's buried gold at Castle Gap in Upton County and look at nineteenth-century engravings of Denton buildings.

Cochran recently sent me a postcard that he thought might interest me. It was probably mailed from El Paso in 1916 or 1917 (the postmark is badly smeared) to a Miss Rosalie Morris, RFD #4, Lonoke, Arkansas. The message reads, "Am going home tomorrow seen the Buck Shot Babies the other day. Write me at Lonoke. I went by on duty and stopped. HEW." Aside from the mysterious reference to the Buck Shot Babies, which may have been a vaudeville act, the written message holds little for the historian. It is the other side of the card that is of interest.

The card's obverse, the side that usually has a picture of a hotel with an "x" marked by a window and "My Room" written above it, has the text of a poem printed on it. The title is "Goin' Home" and there are five stanzas. The first reads

Won't you tell us, Mr. Wilson
Why it is you keep us here
When the border seems so quiet

And there's nothing more to fear?
We don't want to see 'Chewawa'
And we're tired of eating sand
Send us back to Pensyltucky
Where there ain't no Rio Grande

The other four are in the same vein, the last one ending

For we're tired of endless drillin'
And the same old army chow,
Send us home for something fillin'
Mr. Wilson, do it Now!

Below the last line is the name of the author, Wm. Hervey Allen. The card was printed by the W. W. Horne Company, El Paso, Texas.

The card would seem to be an ordinary expression in doggerel verse of the same homesick soldier's complaint that has echoed down through the centuries, except for two things: the references to Mr. Wilson and the Rio Grande and the El Paso imprint tie the poem to the Mexican border troubles of 1916, and the signature below the poem, "Wm. Hervey Allen," is that of a major twentieth-century American literary figure.

William Hervey Allen, better known to his readers as Hervey Allen, was the author of the blockbuster novel *Anthony Adverse*, a historical novel set during the Napoleonic Wars that was a July 1933 Book-of-the-Month Club selection and sold three and a half million copies. Allen's first appearance in print was a forty-six-page booklet entitled *Ballads of the Border: The Weakling and Other Pictures of the Mobilization*, printed in El Paso in 1916 by the McMath Printing Company. It is so rare that I have never seen a copy, but I will bet dollars to doughnuts, as they said in 1916, that "Goin' Home" is one of the poems in it.

William Hervey Allen was born in Pittsburgh, Pennsylvania, in 1889 and graduated from the University of Pittsburgh in 1915. According to his biographer, Stuart Knee, he was a great admirer of Woodrow Wilson, and when Wilson called up the Pennsylvania National Guard to protect the Mexican border Allen joined up as a second lieutenant in the Eighteenth Pennsylvania Infantry and was shipped off to El Paso, where he spent six months camping in the sand. The tone of the poem on the post card indicates he was quickly disillusioned with both Wilson and military life, as well as with West Texas. He was even further disillusioned by combat with the same unit in France during World War I, from which he returned gassed and shell-shocked. He first gained national recognition for his war poem, "Blindman," published in the *North American Review* in 1919.

Allen's reputation as a poet was further enhanced when he moved to Charleston, South Carolina, in 1920 to teach in an exclusive boy's school. There he collaborated with Dubose Heyward, the future author of *Porgy and Bess,* to produce *Carolina Chansons* (1922), a volume of poems about the contemporary South that is considered by some to mark the beginning of the Southern literary renaissance. This was followed in 1926 by a biography of Edgar Allan Poe and in 1929 by *Sarah Simon,* a long poetic work set in the Caribbean. None of the reviews of these publications mentioned *Ballads of the Border.*

In 1933 Allen's behemoth novel *Anthony Adverse* was released by Farrar and Rinehart. Its 1,224 pages of purple prose tracked the swashbuckling adventures of its orphan hero across Europe, Africa, and the Americas as he seeks solace and peace in a war-torn, materialistic world. One reviewer pointed out that it was so long that it offered three weeks' entertainment for three dollars. The novel spoke to the concerns of Depression-era Americans and was a smashing success, the most popular novel of the decade. In

1936 it was made into a film with Fredric March, Olivia de Havilland, and Claude Rains.

In the penultimate chapter of the novel, *Anthony Adverse* has found his life's love in Mexico and takes her north across the Rio Grande to marry her in the chapel at Ysleta Mission. One wonders if, as Hervey Allen penned the lines about the newlyweds' journey through "forests of blooming yuccas, the candelabra of the gods, hung with delicate white bells as though for a wilderness festival of lilies," he remembered his miserable six months in camp along the banks of that same river.

October 6, 2011

✣ 52 ✣

REMEMBERING BRYAN WOOLLEY

I WAS JUST getting ready to leave the house for church last Sunday morning when I got an email from El Paso writer Marcia Hatfield Daudistel telling me that our friend Bryan Woolley had died in Dallas on Friday. Woolley was a Fort Davis boy who wrote one of the best novels about small-town adolescence I know of, *Time and Place*, set in a West Texas town, a thinly disguised Fort Davis. It is, in my opinion, right up there with Larry McMurtry's *The Last Picture Show*, and that is saying a bunch. During his career, Woolley won myriad awards for literary achievement: a Golden Spur Award from the Western Writers of America, a PEN Western Literary Award for Journalism, a Berea College W. D. Weatherford Award for nonfiction, the University of Texas's Stanley Walker Journalism Award (twice); the Texas Headliner Award for outstanding journalism (four times); and four separate awards from the Texas Institute of Letters.

Woolley was born on an Eastland County farm in 1937, but his family moved to Fort Davis when he was very young and lived in the big adobe house on the corner of Court Avenue and Buckeye Street now owned by Marty and Yana Davis. His mother, who had family ties here, served as Jeff Davis County Clerk for many years, and his grandmother taught in our public school. Woolley went all the way through elementary and high school here. He was our hometown boy. When my wife and I first started looking for a house here fifteen years ago, our real estate agent pointed out the Davis's house to us as "the house where Bryan Woolley grew up."

BRYAN WOOLLEY

Woolley's childhood here shaped his writing and his career. When he was a sophomore in high school he won an honorable mention in an *El Paso Times* essay contest for a paper about soil conservation, "a subject about which I knew nothing," he later wrote. The next year the school principal recommended him for a job as the Fort Davis stringer for the *El Paso Times.* Stringers reported local news and were paid fifteen cents a column inch for stories the paper used. Woolley got the job; his first story was about a chicken house fire put out by our volunteer fire department, which the *Times* did not use.

Woolley placed himself under the tutelage of Justice of the Peace Barry Scobee, a former journalist, who showed him how to write feature stories, and within a few months his features about rural life, old timers ("geezers and geezerettes," he called them), and Davis Mountains cowboys and ranchers were appearing with some regularity in the *Times.* When he graduated from Fort Davis High School in 1955, he went to El Paso and got a job on the staff of the *Times.* He started as a photographer's assistant, developing film at $1.00 an hour, but he soon worked his way to the sports desk, taking telephone reports about Friday night high-school football games from stringers and writing them up into stories. Woolley nearly got fired the first month for writing a lengthy and detailed story about a high school game in New Mexico and leaving out the score, but he survived and stayed with the paper until he graduated from Texas Western College at twenty-one and got married to his high school sweetheart, a Marfa girl.

Woolley's path to full-time journalism and literary fame was not straightforward. His fiancée told him that being a newspaper reporter was not a respectable job and that she would not marry him if he stayed with the *Times.* Over the next nine years he taught high school English, worked as a bank teller and on a seismograph crew, and spent time in two graduate schools, including Harvard Divinity School. The marriage ended, and Woolley took a job as a correspondent for the Associated Press in Tulsa. He spent the next fifty years as a journalist, working in Anniston, Alabama; Louisville, Kentucky; and, since 1976, in Dallas, where he wrote features for the *Dallas Times-Herald* and the *Dallas Morning News*. He retired from the *Morning News* in 2006 but still contributed occasional articles to the paper.

Woolley was an extremely versatile writer. His forte was finely honed short portraits of people or places, usually originating as feature assignments, but he also published four novels, two children's books, a nonfiction book about coal miners in Kentucky, a travel book, and numerous short stories. For my money *Time and Place* is his masterpiece. Woolley once told me he did not like the title but he had learned to live with it. He wanted to call the book *The Polio Year*, but his publishers, E. P. Dutton, decided that no one would buy a book with the name of a disease in the title. Woolley pointed out to them that Albert Camus's *The Plague* and Alexander Solzhenitzyn's *Cancer Ward* had done pretty well, but they were adamant, and when the book came out in 1977 it was called *Time and Place*.

The book was inspired by the ordeal and courage of one of Woolley's boyhood friends, Albert Fryer, whose parents, Bill and Vivian Fryer, owned the Fort Davis Drug Store. Fryer got polio at the age of fourteen from swimming in a stock tank here. He survived, but he was badly crippled and died much too young. But *Time and Place* is about far more than illness and youthful courage. It is about how the past shapes the present, about conflicts between Anglos and Mexicans, about how adolescents learn to become adults. The setting, a town which is disguised under the name Fort Appleby, is so obviously Fort Davis that Woolley, in the preface to the 1985 TCU Press edition, wrote that he wondered why he bothered to change the name.

Woolley was a big, shambling man, with long, unkempt hair, glasses, and a scraggly, short beard. He looked like a perpetually inquisitive bear, and he had an air of eternal innocence. Unlike many writers, he was modest, sweet-natured, and completely inept at self-promotion, which is probably why his books are not better known. He loved Fort Davis and the Davis Mountains. He was here about two years ago with his two grown sons. My wife and I had them to lunch, and he told us, "I'm here to show my boys where I want my ashes scattered." He'll be here soon.

January 15, 2015

IV.

COOKS, PHOTOGRAPHERS, POETS, AND OTHERS

❖ 53 ❖

OUR FOUNDING FOODS

Jane Tennant with S.G.B. Tennant Jr.,
Our Founding Foods: Classics from the First Century of American Celebrity Cookbooks.
Minocqua, Wisconsin: Willow Creek Press, 2008.

THE OTHER NIGHT I found myself slicing a pocket in a two-and-a-half pound slab of flank steak, stuffing it with dressing made from bread crumbs, celery, and onions, rolling the whole thing up and tying it with a string, and braising it in beef stock for an hour. I was trying out a recipe for something called Fashionable Flank Steak Roll from Lydia Maria Child's cookbook *The Frugal Housewife, Dedicated to Those Who Are Not Afraid of Economy,* published in Boston in 1832. It may have been fashionable, but it was a tad dry. It would have been improved by a bit of bacon fat stuffed into the pocket with the dressing, but I suppose frugal New England housewives who were not afraid of economy might have regarded bacon as an extravagance. Instead I should probably have made the okra, chicken, shrimp, and sausage gumbo from Mary Randolph's *The Virginia Housewife,* published in Baltimore in 1824. Mary Randolph came from a tradition of generous plantation cooking and was far more interested in flavor than frugality.

Both of these recipes have been gathered under one cover along with over two hundred others from historic American cookbooks by my friend Jane Tennant and published under the title *Our Founding Foods* (Willow Creek Press, $16.95). The recipes are taken from forty-two cookbooks used in America and published between 1615 and 1880. Tennant has modified some of them for modern kitchens, translating phrases like "a pinch of ginger" and "enough salt" into teaspoons and tablespoons and occasionally adding ingredients not available to the original cooks, such as tomatoes and canned chicken stock. The book is chock full of things that I would like to try, such as Chicken Pie with Short Bean Crust, from Mrs. Esther Wilson's *1877 Buckeye Cookery* (the crust is made from a white bean dough) and Uncle Jimmy Matthews's Authentic Brunswick Stew from Marion Harland's *Common Sense in the Household* (1873). Harland calls for two cut-up squirrels in the stew, but Tennant says "chicken can also be used." I'd prefer it with squirrel. The range of recipes is generally well-balanced among main courses, fish, soups, vegetables, breads, and desserts, although forty-nine dessert recipes do seem somewhat excessive. Perhaps Americans have always had a sweet tooth. There is also a section called "Etcetera," which includes Cherry Wine and Epicure's Wow Wow Sauce (mushroom catsup, mashed anchovies, red wine, cayenne pepper, and horseradish all figure among the ingredients).

What makes Tennant's book so enjoyable is that it is far more than a collection of recipes. It is also an essay about American cookbooks and the women who wrote them. Tennant, an Englishwoman and an Oxford graduate who now lives in a Norman castle in the brush country of Karnes County, Texas (more about that later), told me that she first got to looking at cookbooks because she was interested in women's history (she read modern history at Oxford's St. Anne's College), and she was intrigued by the women who wrote cookbooks in the eighteenth and nineteenth centuries. "Amelia Simmons, who wrote the first American cookbook, published in 1796, described herself in the preface as an illiterate orphan," Tennant told me. "Mary Randolph, who wrote *The Virginia Housewife*, was just the opposite. She was a Virginia aristocrat—her brother married Thomas Jefferson's daughter—but her husband was a wipe-out and she had to run a boarding house to survive. Lydia Maria Child was an abolitionist, a reformer with a mission, and so was Catherine Beecher, who wrote *A Treatise on Domestic Economy* in 1841. They were all fascinating women."

Jane Tennant is a fascinating woman herself. She grew up in the market town of Abingdon, Oxfordshire, where MG automobiles used to be made, and started cooking as a child. When she graduated from Oxford, she got a job as a chef and personal assistant to Barbara Castle, an English Labour politician and cabinet minister with a reputation for fiery oratory (her autobiography is called *Fighting All the Way*). After Tennant came to the States in 1982 she was a personal chef to the San Francisco grande dame Miriam Gerstler Wornum. In 1985 she married Sidney Gail Borden Tennant Jr., a fifth-generation Texan and a sportsman whose passion for hunting, fishing, and cooking has resulted in a series of popular wild game cookbooks, published under the collective title *Wild at the Table*. After their marriage they built a home on a Tennant family ranch in Karnes County, designed by Austin architect Stanley Walker. A four-story battlemented tower has a wine cellar in the basement, and an adjacent wing has a large kitchen in which she and her husband cook together. She tells me that she prepares breads, desserts, and salads, and he does the main dishes. They have two daughters, one in college and one in high school, who both recently told their mother that they wanted to learn to cook.

Tennant did the research for *Our Founding Foods* by collecting cookbooks, and her bibliography contains seventy-three entries, ranging from Gervase Markham's *The English Huswife*, published in London in 1615, to the *Melrose Plantation Cookbook*, published in New Orleans in 1956. America's ethnic patchwork is represented in her book by recipes selected from Encarnacion

Pinedo's *El Cocinero Espanol* (California, 1898); Gustav Peters's *Die Geschichte Hausfrau* (Pennsylvania, 1848); Onoto Watama's *Chinese-Japanese Cook Book* (Illinois, 1914); Lafcadio Hearn's *La Cuisine Creole* (Louisiana, 1885); and Esther Levy's *Jewish Cookery Book* (Pennsylvania, 1871). The bibliography also includes something called *The Confederate Receipt Book: A Compilation of Over One Hundred Receipts, Adapted to the Times*, published in Richmond in 1863, which makes one think of okra-seed coffee and tea made from meadow hay, but perhaps fortunately no recipes "adapted to the times" are included in the book. Actually, the only problem with *Our Founding Foods* is that each recipe in it makes you want to go find the book it was taken from and see what else is there.

Well, I'm off to go find a fresh eel with which to make Merrimack Eel Pie, from Hannah Glasse's *The Art of Cooking Made Plain* (1805). If I can't find that perhaps I'll get a five-pound shad and do the Schuykill Planked Shad from Amelia Simmons's *American Cookery* (1796). Thank you, Jane Tennant.

May 22, 2008

✣ 54 ✣

HILLINGDON RANCH

David K. Langford and Lorie Woodward Cantu,
Hillingdon Ranch: Four Seasons, Six Generations.
College Station: Texas A&M University Press, 2013.

DAVID K. LANGFORD used to make his living photographing other people's livestock. If you wanted a gorgeous photo of your prize bull or your quarter horse for an ad in *Western Horseman* or *The Western Livestock Journal*, Langford was your man. Over the years he widened the scope of his photography to include Western wildlife and landscapes, and his work has appeared in national magazines such as *Smithsonian, Outdoor Life, Field and Stream*, and *Sports Afield*. He is one of Texas's best-known wildlife photographers.

Lorie Woodward Cantu is a professional agricultural writer who was once the editor of a journal that I remember from childhood as the *Brahman Breeder-Feeder*, subscribed to by my Brahman-raising great-uncles; now called the *Brahman Journal*, it is the official publication of the American Brahman Breeders Association. More recently, she was the official spokesperson for the Texas Department of Agriculture. She has a remarkable talent for distilling raw data and statistics into compelling stories and for translating specialists' jargon into ordinary English.

Langford and Cantu have recently combined their talents to produce a beautiful book, *Hillingdon Ranch: Four Seasons, Six Generations* (Texas A&M Press, $35.00), about land stewardship over six generations on a Texas Hill Country ranch. The thirteen-thousand-acre ranch near Comfort was founded by Langford's great-grandfather, the English-born San Antonio architect Alfred Giles, who purchased his first land there in 1885. At one time Giles commuted from the ranch to San Antonio by railroad, being driven to the station in Comfort in a buggy. He took two homing pigeons with him, releasing one when he got to San Antonio so that his family would know that he had arrived safely, and the other when he started home so that the buggy would be at the Comfort station when he arrived.

The ranch is now managed by Langford's cousins, Alfred Giles's grandson Robin Giles and his wife, Carol, and their son Grant and his wife, Misty. Portions are now owned by other family members, but Robin and Grant Giles, through a series of annual agreements with forty-odd cousins, manage the acreage as a unit, raising cattle, sheep, and goats and showing a profit most years. They do most of the ranch work themselves, living in the stone house that Alfred Giles built. The house is not air-conditioned. Robin Giles told Lorie Cantu that "air conditioning makes it too hard to get back outside and do what needs to be done."

The key to the Gileses' successful management is careful stewardship of the ranch's natural resources. Their animals, says Robin Giles, are not raised for the show ring but bred to fit into the environment without unduly stressing it or them. "We select the ones that are most efficient, most healthy, produce the most with the least input, and we live with them," he told Cantu. "We don't chase after someone else's vision of the 'perfect' animal."

Hillingdon Ranch is organized around life on the ranch during the four seasons, with each section illustrated with Langford's photographs. Most Texas photographic books are just that, books of pretty photographs, but I learned something I didn't know in each section from both Langford's photographs and Cantu's prose. For instance, in the "Spring" section, which deals with lambing, kidding, and calving, I learned that nannies are careless mothers and ewes are not. Cantu quotes Robin Giles as saying, "In the first twenty-four hours, nannies pay close attention to their kids, but then they're ready to go sight-seeing. Goats have a big agenda, and in a big pasture they have to go and see and do everything. . . . They can have trouble finding their kids again." Ewes, on the other hand, "have a one-track mind. They think of nothing but their lambs." The "Summer" section is full of information about grazing; the "Fall" section about feeding. Cantu describes how the Gileses use a feed truck to manage their livestock, pointing out that a feed truck can gather all of the cattle in a one thousand-acre pasture in ninety minutes, a job that it would take several men on horseback two days to accomplish with dogs. Langford's photographs illustrate both processes, the November afternoon sun turning the pasture grass gold in his shot of a cowboy moving cattle on horseback with a dog. Part of the "Winter " section deals with the wool clip and the Gileses' success at achieving a balance between wool production and lamb production, reducing the wool clip per sheep to increase the number of lambs born but then increasing the fineness of the wool by selective breeding to keep the wool profit up. If I were going to give someone a book to explain how a modern ranch is run, this is the book I would give them.

If *Hillingdon Ranch* has an underlying theme it is balance. Robin Giles says, "Ranching comes down to managing relationships. You've got to maintain the relationship between family and friends, you've got to sustain the relationship between you and the land, you've got to recognize the relationship between all of the natural resources, you've got to balance the successes of the past with the challenges of the future." Maintaining balance requires constant flexibility. The most astonishing example in the book is the case of a cousin who is a mountain bike enthusiast and has criss-crossed his section of the ranch with biking trails. He and his wife host organized biking events that involve as many as 1,500 people coming on the ranch as participants and spectators, but gates with automatic closing devices, carefully explained rules, and superb people-management skills keep the crowds compatible with the livestock. One of the rules is "If you touch a new-born kid you have to take it home and raise it." Langford himself conducts wildlife photography workshops on the property that attract participants from all over the world.

When I asked David Langford why he thought the Giles family had been such careful stewards of the land for so long, he said, "I think it has to do with continuity of ownership. When you've been the recipient of a great gift like this ranch you want to pass it on intact." With *Hillingdon Ranch: Four Seasons, Six Generations* Langford and Cantu have passed that gift on to the public, and at a bargain price, too.

February 6, 2014

✣ 55 ✣

A LONG VIEW SOUTHWEST

J. Frank Dobie and Jim Bones,
A Long View Southwest.
Alpine, Texas: The Goathead Press, 2012.

JIM BONES, who has been making photographs for the Museum of the Big Bend in Alpine for the past few years, has just published a new book, *A Long View Southwest.* It is his eighth book. His color photographs have illustrated a dozen other books and countless magazine articles on natural history and the American landscape over the past forty years. Bones, who has lived in Alpine since 2005, is a nationally known nature photographer.

In *A Long View Southwest,* Bones has juxtaposed some of his finest color photographs of the Southwestern landscape, many of them taken in the Big Bend, with quotations about the Southwest taken from J. Frank Dobie's annotated bibliography, *Guide to the Life and Literature of the Southwest.* Those familiar with that bibliography will recall that Dobie's annotations to the entries are exhaustive and contain much pithy wisdom about the Southwest, and they may also recall that Dobie refused to copyright the book but instead inserted the words "Not copyright in 1942, again not copyright in 1952, anybody is welcome to help himself to any of it in any way" in place of the usual copyright notice. Bones has helped himself, and the result is remarkably apt.

When we talked over coffee at the Sul Ross University Center last week, Bones told me that the book had its genesis in 1972, when he applied for a University of Texas Dobie-Paisano fellowship to spend a year at Dobie's ranch outside Austin, which Dobie left to the university as a writers' retreat. His proposal was to photograph the seasonal changes at the 257-acre ranch and write a book about them. Frank Wardlow, the director of the University of Texas Press who was then in charge of the Dobie-Paisano program, thought that the photography was a fine idea but suggested that John Graves, the best-known writer in Texas, write the words. Bones could hardly refuse. The book was published in 1975 as *Texas Heartland: A Hill Country Year,* with a text by Graves and a "Photographer's Introduction" by Bones.

Bones went on to write and illustrate a series of books that treat the ecology of the Southwest in ever-expanding circles. *Texas Heartland,* he says, is a look at the Hill Country through the fingerprint of the Dobie ranch. His next book, *Texas West of the Pecos* (1981), grew out of his adventures as a boatman for Far Flung Adventures in Terlingua and dealt with the desert through the lens of the Big Bend. A third book, *Rio Grande: Mountains to the Sea* (1985), integrates several regions. He is completing another book with Mary Bones, *Islands of Wildness,* which will deal with all of the major ecological regions of North America. With *A Long View Southwest,* Bones has come full circle, blending Dobie's words with his own photography.

Bones started using a camera early in life. The son of an Air Force officer, he spent his childhood on air bases. He remembers that at the age of seventeen he was arrested at gunpoint by the Air Police on Vandenberg Air Force Base in Lompoc, California, for trying to photograph a Titan ICBM test launch. He had sneaked within the launch perimeter and was spotted by a helicopter while aiming his camera from a foxhole he had prepared. He was later told that the incident had led to the cancellation of the test at a cost of $40 million to the government.

At the University of Texas in the early 1960s, Bones became a student of former Farm Security Administration photographer

Russell Lee. Lee was teaching at the university and, impressed by an exhibit of Bones's photography, hired him as an assistant. Through Lee, Bones met the great nature photographer Eliot Porter, and in 1975 Porter hired Bones as his printer, teaching him the dye-transfer process of color printing. Bones worked in Porter's darkroom in Tesuque, New Mexico, until 1978 and then started teaching photography and dye-transfer printing himself, taking small groups of photographers on field trips all over North America. Eventually, Bones says, he tired of the responsibility of taking people into the field. On one Alaska trip, he recalls, he discovered that one of the participants, a cancer patient, had come with the express purpose of dying in Alaska, and another, a woman, flirted so outrageously with the crew members on the ferry they were travelling on that she involved Bones in a confrontation with a knife-wielding sailor.

In the early 1990s, Bones accepted an assignment from a group in Santa Fe called Seeds of Change, photographing vegetables as illustrations for a book on heirloom seeds. Bones said, "It was the best assignment I ever had. I could photograph the subject and then eat it—fifty varieties of tomatoes!" Through Seeds of Change Bones met Japanese microbiologist and natural farming innovator Masanobu Fukuoka, whom he credits with changing his life. Fukuoka developed a method of restoring abused land with seedballs, marble-sized pellets of clay, compost, and seeds which can be broadcast by hand. Bones became a disciple, and for the past twenty years has propagated the gospel of seedballs. A fine film that he made on the subject, "The Seedball Story," which features three Alpine youngsters, Max Bell, Rachel Sibley, and Mariah Barrick, is available on YouTube.

Bones describes himself as a naturalist, a nineteenth-century word meaning someone who studies the interaction of all nature, rather than specializing in a particular field. He is pessimistic about mankind's efforts to control nature. "We can only work in concert with nature," he told me. "Instead of building seawalls around our coastal cities, we should be encouraging people to migrate to higher ground. Nature always bats last."

When I first knew Jim Bones in the early 1970s, he and his first wife, Ann Matlock, were living in a house in the country west of Austin that was built around a Ford Econoline van. Their bedroom was the body of the van; the van's roof was the floor of the guest room, and one of its sides was the wall of the kitchen. Bones referred to the van's front seat as the television room, the television being the view of the landscape through the windshield. Watching and learning from landscape has become Bones's life's work.

March 7, 2013

✣ 56 ✣

WATT MATTHEWS OF LAMBSHEAD

Laura Wilson, *Watt Matthews of Lambshead.*
Austin: The Texas State Historical Association, 2017.

LAURA WILSON'S book *Watt Matthews of Lambshead* has the best opening sentence of any Texas book that I know of. It is "Watt Matthews is 90 years old and still in charge." Wilson, who is a Dallas-based photographer, was in Marfa last month to talk about her book, which was first published in 1989 by the Texas State Historical Association and has just been rereleased in an updated third edition. The book consists of 102 photographs of rancher Watt Matthews and his cowboys and neighbors on the sixty-five-square mile Lambshead Ranch outside of Albany, Texas, with a text by Wilson, who spent five years taking the pictures. The book is a Texas classic.

As Wilson's text explains, Watt Matthews, who was born in 1899 and died in 1997, was one of the second generation of two interlocked families, the Matthews and the Reynolds, who settled in Shackleford County in the late 1850s, when it was still on the Comanche frontier. Except for four years at Princeton University, he lived on Lambshead all of his life and took over its management in 1941, when his father died. He never married, and though he was a comparatively wealthy man (he was fond of saying "The best cross with a Hereford is a pumpjack"), he slept in a room in the ranch bunkhouse furnished with a single bed, a chair, a bureau, and a bootjack. He spent his life improving the ranch and the breed of cattle it produced, and he earned the respect of every rancher in Texas for his integrity, his sagacity, and his legendary hospitality.

Wilson's photographs catch these qualities perfectly. She is a slim woman in her seventies with finely chiseled features and a precise way of speaking. During her talk at the Crowley Theater she projected memorable images on the screen and commented on them: Watt in the cab of his pickup, his hands on the wheel and a narrow-brimmed, sweat-stained Stetson on his head; six dead coyotes hanging from a dead tree; a thorny thicket of prickly pear; Watt asleep on a narrow bench in the bunkhouse, a packet of letters under his head; a saddled horse standing on the sod roof of a stone-fronted dugout, with a cowboy named Frank Perry posed in front of it. "Watt was a small man. He stood five-foot-six inches, and he had the brims of his hats cut down in proportion to his stature," Wilson told her audience. "Watt spent his life in relentless battle against two implacable foes, mesquite and prickly pear," she said. "Watt was a master of the cat nap," she said. "He could go to sleep anywhere for five or ten minutes and wake up totally refreshed." She spoke about Matthews with such intimacy and sympathy that you would have thought that she had grown up on Lambshead with him, a niece or younger cousin.

I talked with Wilson shortly after her Marfa appearance, and she told me that she was actually born and grew up in New England, in a town called Norwell, Massachusetts, on the South Shore of Massachusetts Bay. Her father, she said, was a Boston insurance executive, but he wanted his children to have the experience of growing up in a small, rural town, so he settled in Norwell and commuted daily to work in Boston. "There were thirty-two people in my high school class," Wilson said, "and only five of us went to college. The rest all found jobs on farms or in shops." She went on to say all of her school friends had horses, and they rode together every day after school. "I still have friends I went to the first grade with," she told me.

Wilson was fascinated with photography as a child and has always taken pictures, first with a Brownie and later with a 35mm Minolta that she got when she was fifteen. "I can remember poring over issues of *U.S. Camera* when I was six. I was fascinated by the war photography, pictures of men on the beach at Normandy. I always knew that I wanted to be a photographer."

Wilson went to the Connecticut College for Women and met her husband, Robert, a Bostonian who was at Dartmouth, while they were both in college. They married in 1963 and moved to Dallas in 1965, when Robert was transferred there by his employer, the Scott Paper Company. "It was a shock to move to Dallas," Wilson told me. "Dallas women were very different from New England women. I would have felt more at home if we had moved to Europe." The Wilsons soon became part of the city's cultural life, however. In 1968 Robert (who died in May 2017) became the managing director of Dallas's educational television station, KERA-TV, and went on to found his own advertising and graphic design firm. Laura found work at the Amon Carter Museum, in neighboring Fort Worth, as an assistant to photographer Richard Avedon on the museum's five-year project to photograph the working people of the West, *In the American West.* Wilson documented this experience in her 2003 book, *Avedon at Work: In the American West.* She has also published a book on the Hutterite communities of Montana and *That Day*, her own take on the diverse people of the West. She is currently working on three more books: one of portraits of writers; one about filmmaking (her three sons, Owen, Luke, and Andrew, are all successful Hollywood actors); and one about Ross Perot Jr.'s industrial park and real estate development, Alliance. All of her projects, she says, are about people.

So how was a born-and-bred New Englander able to empathize with a tough West Texas rancher and his cowboys?

"Watt Matthews was much more like me than Richard Avedon was," Wilson told me. "I grew up with hard-working rural people who had old-fashioned values, and Watt and the people around Albany were just like the people I grew up with. I understood them."

That understanding shows on every page of *Watt Matthews of Lambshead*. I think it also helped Laura Wilson that she has a beautiful smile, and her subjects smiled back at her.

February 8, 2018

✣ 57 ✣

THE WHITE SHAMAN MURAL

Carolyn E. Boyd, *The White Shaman Mural: An Enduring Creation Narrative in the Rock Art of the Lower Pecos.* Austin: University of Texas Press, 2016.

CAROLYN BOYD is a pivotal figure in Texas archaeology. This Galveston-born anthropologist has revolutionized the way we look at prehistoric rock art. She has done that because she first looked at it through the eyes of an artist, not those of an archaeologist.

In 1969 I took a course at the University of Texas from Dr. Bill Newcomb, director of the Texas Memorial Museum and coauthor with Forest Kirkland of *The Rock Art of Texas Indians* (University of Texas Press, 1967). Although the course was in museology, the talk around the seminar table often turned to prehistoric rock art because Newcomb's book had just come out. Newcomb felt that the Indian pictographs that are found on cliffs and in rock shelters all over West Texas were groups of random images associated with shamanistic religion and hunting, accumulated at each site over long periods of time stretching over several thousand years. We did not get to hear Forest Kirkland's opinions because Kirkland, a Dallas artist who did watercolor renderings of about 150 West Texas pictograph sites, died in 1942. His watercolors ended up at the Texas Memorial Museum, and Newcomb's book was a commentary on Kirkland's paintings. Newcomb's random-image theo-

CAROLYN BOYD

ry was shared by most anthropologists who worked with Southwestern rock art in the 1960s.

Carolyn Boyd's recent book, *The White Shaman Mural* (University of Texas Press, 2016), makes that theory forever obsolete. The White Shaman mural is an assemblage of red, yellow, black, and white images twenty-six feet long and thirteen feet high, painted on the back wall of a shallow cave on the east bank of the Pecos River, just upriver from the US 90 bridge over the Pecos. The cave is visible from the bridge if you know where to look. Carolyn Boyd first saw the painting in 1989 and, she told me, instantly realized that it was an intentional composition and not a collection of random images. "It had a structure that anyone who is an artist would have recognized," Boyd said. At the time she was a working artist, running her own gallery in Spring, Texas, and working as a commissioned muralist to put bread on the table. Boyd's mother, Jody Calvin Boyd, was a well-known gallery owner and artist and sometime president of the West Virginia Watercolor Society, and Boyd told me, "I grew up with a paintbrush in my hand."

Ironically, Boyd said, Forest Kirkland had also recognized the compositional nature of some of the pictographs that he copied in the 1930s, but he was an artist with only one year of college and no one in the archaeological world paid any attention to his theories. Boyd did not want her insight into the White Shaman mural to meet the same fate, and she wanted to increase her understanding of the people who created it, so she went back to Texas A&M (she had dropped out after her sophomore year to get married) and got her PhD in anthropology in 1998, writing her dissertation on the rock art of the lower Pecos. She is now on the faculty at Texas State University at San Marcos, and her opinions are listened to with respect by her fellow academics.

Boyd is convinced that the White Shaman mural and other Lower Pecos murals that she has examined are not aggregations of randomly placed images but are "compositionally intricate, highly patterned murals" presenting complex narratives. The White Shaman mural, she argues, is an illustration of a proto-Mesoamerican myth involving a pilgrimage, the slaying of a deer, and the offering of fire to the rising sun. The myth was found among the Aztecs and is still part of the belief system of the Huichol Indians of Mexico's Sierra Madre.

Boyd reached these conclusions after making an intensive study of both Nahua and Huichol mythology and ritual. She explored Huichol mythology through the anthropological literature and Nahua beliefs and practices represented in painted codices that were produced about the time of the Spanish conquest in the early 1500s. Boyd has found similarities between the figures in the codices and the figures painted at the White Shaman site nearly 2,000 years earlier.

Boyd's interpretation was confirmed to her satisfaction in 2010 when a Huichol shaman named Matsihua visited Boyd at the White Shaman site. Boyd told me, "He was accompanied by his son and was traveling in his traditional shaman's embroidered clothing and hat with little balls of yarn dangling from its brim. He went through the Border Patrol checkpoint at Del Rio dressed like that. We spent twenty-four hours together and talked through two interpreters, one translating from Huichol to Spanish and one from Spanish to English. When he saw the mural he started sobbing and said, 'They are all here, all of the great-grandfathers.' He was having a family reunion. That night we had a ceremony and he sang all night."

Boyd has employed the latest types of scientific technology in her analysis of the White Shaman mural, including a hand-held digital microscope that enabled her and her colleagues to capture hundreds of photomicrographs of portions of the painting at fifty to two-hundred power. These photomicrographs enabled her to determine in what order the different layers of paint in the mural were applied. To her astonishment she found that all of the black paint, even the small back dots that ornament larger figures on the periphery of the mural, was laid on first, followed by the red and then the yellow and finally the white. This discovery confirmed beyond all doubt that the mural was the conception of a single artist and was produced all at one time.

In the concluding chapter of her book, Boyd reminds us that the White Shaman mural, and other examples of trans-Pecos rock art, are stories told by ancient artists about basic truths of life. "The method of reading that story," she writes, "was handed down from generation to generation, so that anyone who understood the grammar could read the painting. Then at some point in time everyone with that special knowledge moved on, and the message of the White Shaman mural went into a very long period of dormancy." Boyd's instincts as an artist, combined with her skills as an anthropologist, have revived the mural's message for us, and by doing this she has immeasurably enhanced our knowledge of the people who preceded us in the Big Bend.

August 31, 2017

✣ 58 ✣

HOME GROUND

Barry Lopez, *Home Ground: Language for an American Landscape.*
San Antonio: Trinity University Press, 2006.

When I lived in New Mexico I had a friend named Benito Cordova who was one of the most remarkable people I have ever met. He was part Hispanic and part Navajo, and he had his own way of going about things. He had never traveled far from New Mexico, but he had a vigorous curiosity about the rest of the world. One day he and I were driving across the sun-bleached, broken country south of Albuquerque, where the road dips down into wide dry arroyos, and he turned to me and said, "Lonn, what do they call arroyos in the East?" That stumped me. I had never thought about arroyos in the East, and after a minute I told him that they didn't have arroyos in the East. He looked at me as though he was disappointed by my ignorance but was too polite to say so and changed the subject.

Several years later I was driving in the mountains of western Virginia and crossed a small, rock-strewn dry gulch cut into the side of a fairly steep hill. If it had been in New Mexico it would have been an arroyo. There was a sign on the bridge over it that said "Stewart's Draft." There was the answer to Benito's question. In Highland County, Virginia, arroyos were called drafts. For a number of years I thought I had solved the problem of what arroyos were called in the East. But I recently discovered that the term "draft" is only used in a few counties along the Virginia-West Virginia border and in the mountains of western Pennsylvania. It is an extreme localism.

I made this discovery in a wonderful book called *Home Ground*, edited by Barry Lopez and published recently by Trinity University Press in San Antonio. *Home Ground* is an encyclopedia of terms employed by different kinds of Americans to describe geographic features, terms like bayou and hassock and atarque and mima mound. The features described in the book range in size from a tsegi, which on the Navajo Reservation in New Mexico and Arizona can be a canyon thirty miles long, to feeding craters, the little pock marks that sheep make in the Montana snow when they nose it aside to get at the grass underneath. But this book is not really about geography; it is about language, and the endlessly inventive ways that people have coined words and phrases to describe what they see around them. The forty-odd contributors are not academic geographers but writers, people like novelist Barbara Kingsolver and essayist Arturo Longoria and historian William duBuys and naturalist Terry Tempest Williams, who have written feelingly about particular places. So *Home Ground* falls more into the realm of literature than science, more under the descriptive rubric of "sense of place" than "geography." If I were a librarian I'd be hard put to know where to shelve it.

The contributors, even though they are not academics, are aware of the academic explanations and controversies concerning certain geographic terms, but they bring an added dimension to their entries. In discussing bar ditches, for instance, Stephen Graham Jones offers the generally accepted explanation that the term comes from "borrow ditch," meaning that dirt is taken from the ditches during construction to build up the road surface between them, but he adds the information that they harbor rattlesnakes, who like to get up against the warm edges of the asphalt pavement, and he throws in a quotation from Texas novelist Elmer Kelton. He does not include my friend George Dolan's explanation that they are called bar ditches because of all the beer cans that can be found in them.

Similarly, in Barry Lopez's entry on "shinnery," Lopez explains that this word is used in eastern New Mexico and the Texas Panhandle to describe thickets of Harvard oak, Vassey oak, and Mohr oak, but then he veers off into other terms used to describe impassable thickets, comes back to the folk etymology that "shinnery" and "shin oak" are so called because you crack your shins on the branches when you try to push through them, and winds up by employing the tactful phrase "by a very different line of reckoning" to say that shinnery probably derives from the French word *cheniere*, used in Louisiana to mean a hummock in a swamp covered with a dense growth of oak (*chene* in French).

One achievement of *Home Ground* is to quickly disabuse the reader of the notion that our country was settled by Englishmen who landed at Plymouth and Jamestown and rolled inexorably westward to the Pacific, as most of our history textbooks would have us believe. The number of French and Spanish landscape terms employed across the country is simply staggering. The Spanish words that have attached themselves to features dealing with irrigation alone run from *acequia* (in Texas and New Mexico) to *zanja* (in California) and include *atarque*, the small reservoir behind an irrigation dam; *chaco*, the irrigated land near a village; and *sangrias*, the little ditches that carry water from the main acequia into the fields. These words and others like them pin down the vast quarter of North America that was explored and settled by the Spanish while the English were still clinging to the Atlantic coast. In the same way, words like *ronde*, a circular prairie; *marais*, a marsh; *palouse*, grassy hills; *coteau*, a ridge overlooking a plain; and *bois brule* (sometimes rendered by English speakers as bob ruly), a burned-over area in the woods, all of which are found strewn over the landscape from Illinois to Oregon, remind us of how far French fur-traders penetrated into North America and that, had the English not won the Seven Years War, we might all be speaking French.

Over near College Station there is a little creek called Cow Bayou. It was originally called Rio Caballo, but to the Anglo settlers who pushed up the Brazos to it in the 1840s the word "*caballo*" sounded like "cow bayou," and that's how they wrote it down on their maps, employing what I always thought was a French word from Louisiana meaning a slow-moving stream. But *Home Ground* tells me that the word "bayou" is actually Choctaw, from *bayuk*, a small stream. Layers upon layers, just like our nation.

January 25, 2007

✣ 59 ✣

AUTHENTIC TEXAS

Marcia Hatfield Daudistel and Bill Wright,
Authentic Texas: The People of the Big Bend.
Austin: University of Texas Press, 2013.

MARCIA HATFIELD DAUDISTEL is a small woman, but she vibrates with energy and can talk a blue streak. She is the kind of person who can pretty much take over a table for four in a restaurant and hold everyone's attention through dessert. She is also a superb interviewer and can get people to tell her things they would not tell their own spouses, and weep while they are doing it. People instinctively trust her, perhaps because she appears somewhat vulnerable herself. She would have made a great war correspondent. I can see her as the Martha Gellhorn of Afghanistan, interviewing battle-hardened GIs and Afghani mothers with equal success.

Instead, she has spent most of the past year in the Big Bend, interviewing people about why they live here and what is special to them about this place. Daudistel is doing this because she is working with Bill Wright on a book about the Big Bend called *Authentic Texas: The People of the Big Bend*, which will be published next year by the University of Texas Press. Wright photographs the interviewees and Daudistel talks with them and then writes up the interviews. Wright has already done one book of Big Bend photographs, *Portraits of the Desert: Bill Wright's Big Bend*, published by the University of Texas Press in 1998, and this one promises to be even better (full disclosure: my wife and I are among those who have been photographed and interviewed by Wright and Daudistel).

Daudistel lives in El Paso, where her husband, Howard Daudistel, is senior executive vice-president of the University of Texas at El Paso. She grew up in Shreveport, Louisiana, but has spent most of her adult life in Texas. She told me that she moved to El Paso in 1983 "as a corporate wife in another life." She went back to school at UTEP and got an honors degree in English and a divorce at about the same time, so she took a job as an office manager for the university's press, Texas Western Press. The press had a very small staff, and Daudistel ended up doing sales and publicity for them as well as running their office.

"I started out by taking a carload of books to Santa Fe and Albuquerque and hitting all of the bookstores there," Daudistel told me over dinner in Marfa recently. "The only book that we had in print that I thought anyone there would buy was Marc Simmons's *Murder on the Santa Fe Trail*, but we also published a Southwestern Studies Series of pamphlets and a Science Series, and I took those along, too. One of the titles in the Science Series was *The Ashmunella Rhyssa (Dall) Complex*, which I can only describe as a sex manual for snails. I ended up getting orders for $10,000 worth of books in one day. That was more books than Texas Western Press sold during the entire previous year. No one from the press had ever made a sales call before, anywhere."

Daudistel could sell iceboxes to Eskimos. Once, she told me, she was trying to persuade the bookstore at UCLA to order copies of Jim Bob Tinsley's *The Puma: Legendary Lion of the Americas*, a Texas Western Press publication. The jacket flap had a photograph of the author proudly standing by a dead puma hanging from an overhead hook. The book buyer was an animal rights enthusiast who winced at the photo and said, "I don't believe that's for us." Daudistel said, "They're dancing." The buyer ordered five copies.

Daudistel eventually became the associate director of Texas Western Press, a position that put her in constant touch with every writer in El Paso and steeped her in that city's long bicultural literary history. She put that knowledge to good use when TCU Press invited her to edit *Literary El Paso*, a 570-page anthology of prose and poetry about El Paso. In her introduction to that volume she describes El Paso as "the dark-eyed exotic stranger abducted into Texas by the treaty of Guadalupe Hidalgo," the best explanation of that city's mystique that I have ever heard. She also demonstrates a fine appreciation for the effect of the Mexican Revolution on El Paso's history, pointing out, for instance, that Mariano Azuela finished his classic novel of the revolution, *Los de Abajo*, in an apartment on Oregon Street. Her anthology also acknowledges the role of El Paso writers in the Chicano movement of the 1960s and 70s by including pieces by Ruben Salazar and Mario T. Garcia, as well as by my favorite Hispanic Texan writer who no one knows is either Hispanic or Texan, John Rechy. I once lent Rechy's 1963 autobiographical novel about a gay hustler, *City of the Night*, to a Fort Worth friend who returned it the same day, saying he was afraid to have it in his car for fear he would have a wreck and someone would find it there. Daudistel includes an excerpt from a yet-to-be-published Rechy book, *Autobiography: A Novel*, in which he reveals that his Scottish grandfather was Porfirio Diaz's personal physician, to my mind a typical El Pasoan antecedent.

Daudistel's latest book, *Grace and Gumption: The Women of El Paso*, published a month ago by TCU Press, is a compilation of pieces by women writers about El Paso women who helped to shape the city, women like librarian Maud Sullivan, who presided over El Paso's public library for twenty-five years and fostered the careers of a clutch of El Paso writers and artists including Rechy,

BILL
MARCIA

Tom Lea, and José Cisneros. Daudistel's own contribution to the volume, besides editing it, is a chapter written with archivist Susan Goodman Novick about Los Comadres, an El Paso women's club that traces its origin to a group of matrons who grew up together in El Paso in the 1890s. In the 1930s the group decided to have quarterly meetings to renew their girlhood friendships and pass their stories of those days on to their daughters, nieces, and daughters-in-law. The club is now in its third generation, and its members have preserved a significant chunk of the oral history of El Paso. I think it is highly significant that Daudistel, a consummate oral historian, chose this group to write about. If she knocks on your door in the next month, let her in. You will have the time of your life talking to her.

December 8, 2011

✣ 60 ✣

CAPTURING NATURE

Patsy Pittman Light, *Capturing Nature: The Cement Sculpture of Dionicio Rodriguez*. College Station: Texas A&M University Press, 2007.

VISITORS to San Antonio sometimes comment on a peculiar bus-stop shelter on Broadway just north of its intersection with Hildebrand, in front of one of the gates to the campus of the University of the Incarnate Word. At first glance it looks like something out of a Mexican jungle, a thatched roof supported by three thick tree trunks rising from a floor of half-sawn logs, with backless split-log benches around the base of each tree trunk. Except that the whole thing is made out of textured and colored concrete.

Not far away in Brackenridge Park is a footbridge that resembles a long arbor. Thirty-three pairs of tree trunks face each other on either side of a plank floor, their branches interlocking above, each trunk joined to the next by log handrails. The logs are riddled with knotholes and insect borings and have patches where the bark has been stripped from them. The tree trunks, the branches, the handrails, and the plank floor are all concrete.

Just up Hildebrand from the bus shelter is a small city park called Miraflores Park, all that is left of a fifteen-acre private garden built in the 1920s by Dr. Aureliano Urrutia, a San Antonio physician whose mansion was nearby. One of the gates to the park is an archway cut into a hollow tree, which leads to twelve crosscut log steps that curve downward into the park. Once more, all concrete.

These monumental curiosities are all the work of Dionicio Rodriguez, a native of Mexico who was a master of the concrete-working technique known in Spanish as *trabajo rustico* (rustic work) and in French as *faux bois* (imitation wood). Rodriguez came to San Antonio from Mexico in 1924 to work on Dr. Urrutia's garden, went on to ornament other parts of San Antonio and to jobs in several other cities in Texas, and traveled with his crew to execute projects across the country until his death in 1955. His somewhat bizarre work is in the aesthetic tradition of miniature golf courses, but it is technically perfect, and it has always attracted the attention of fans whose initial reaction is usually, "Who in the world would do something like that?"

Now that question has been answered in a new book by Patsy Pittman Light, *Capturing Nature: The Cement Sculpture of Dionicio Rodriguez*, published by Texas A&M Press. Light, who is an ardent historic preservationist, became fascinated by Rodriguez's bus stop shelter and Brackenridge Park bridge when she moved to San Antonio forty-five years ago. In 1995 some of Rodriguez's work at San Antonio's Alamo Cement Company headquarters, including a 125-foot long fence incorporating twenty varieties of tree bark and a fountain ornamented with concrete cactus plants, was threatened with destruction when the property they were on was sold to a developer to become a shopping center. The San Antonio Conservation Society stepped in to save them, and Light wrote National Register of Historic Places nominations for them. The research that she did for those nominations started her on a ten-year quest for information about the mysterious Rodriguez, and *Capturing Nature* is the result.

Light's research led her not only to examples of Rodriguez's work all over the country but to some very peculiar clients. In Port Arthur, Texas, she learned about tugboat captain Ambrose

Eddingston, who hired Rodriguez to build ornamental structures in an apartment complex he was developing. Eddingston gave Rodriguez 5,000 conch shells that he had imported from his native Cayman Islands, and Rodriguez used them to build a shell-encrusted wall and gate and a grotto called the Cave of a Thousand Sounds whose interior is covered with conch shells. In North Little Rock, Arkansas, she encountered real estate developer Justin Matthews, who hired Rodriguez to ornament a park in one of his developments with a full-sized nineteenth-century stone mill, whose concrete machinery is powered by a ten-thousand-pound concrete waterwheel. In Memphis she found out about Clovis Hinds, a cemetery developer who, inspired by Los Angeles's Forest Lawn Cemetery, retained Rodriguez to create cement representations of Biblical sites, including Abraham's Oak, the Cave of Machpelah, and the Pool of Hebron, as well as the non-Biblical Annie Laurie Wishing Chair at his Memorial Park Cemetery.

Rodriguez did not draw up plans or keep written records of his work, so Light was dependent on oral sources for information about his techniques and methods. She was able to find several men who had worked with him, including his great-nephew Carlos Cortes, who continued the tradition of Rodriguez's work in San Antonio. But her most valuable source was Rodriguez's niece Manuela Vargas Theall, who had traveled with Rodriguez and his crew in the 1930s and had kept a box of photographs and correspondence. The man who emerges from these interviews is a dapper, somewhat vain, exacting, and secretive craftsman, who was prosperous enough to buy a new car every year during the Depression. According to his niece, Rodriguez always wore a three-piece suit and a dress shirt with cufflinks and a tie. When he went to work, he took off his coat and pulled on coveralls and galoshes. His crew built the armatures for his structures and applied the first layers of concrete under his direction, but it was

Rodriguez who applied the final layer and added the color and the texture. He mixed his colors in the trunk of his car or in a little tent, and would not let anyone come near him while he was doing it, fearful that one of his crew might learn his techniques and go into competition with him. When he got old, he paid neighborhood boys a penny each to pluck out the white hairs from his head.

Rodriguez's skill with concrete and color enabled him to create unique monuments that rank with Sam Rodia's Watts Towers, Leonard Knight's Salvation Mountain, and other visionary environments. When Patsy Light first contacted Manuela Vargas Theall, Manuela said, "I always hoped that my uncle would be famous." Now, thanks to Light's research and the beautiful color photographs which illustrate her book, he will be.

April 3, 2008

✣ 61 ✣

JOEL NELSON: COWBOY POET AND NATIONAL HERITAGE FELLOW

ONE OF OUR neighbors, Joel Nelson of Alpine, has just been named a National Heritage Fellow by the National Endowment for the Arts. National Heritage Fellows, only three hundred of which have been named since the program started in 1982, are chosen for their artistic excellence and their contributions to their respective artistic traditions. They receive a lifetime appointment and a $25,000 award. Nelson was selected for his talent as a reciter and writer of cowboy poetry and for his contributions over the years to the Texas Cowboy Poetry Gathering at Sul Ross State University, which is the second-oldest such gathering in the United States. If the National Endowment for the Arts gave an award for all-around cowboying, Nelson would have won that, too; that is what he has done most of his life.

I talked with Nelson the other day over a cup of coffee at the Bread and Breakfast in Alpine. He is a small man in his early sixties with a gray thatch of a moustache, an unlined face, and a quiet and thoughtful manner. He told me that he was born and grew up in Seymour, Texas, where his father was a cowboy for the Boone Ranch and later a Baylor County deputy sheriff. "I grew up in the old rock jail in Seymour," he said. He went on his first cattle drive at the age of six when he helped his father and the Boone Ranch crew move a herd of steers to a shipping point on the railroad between Seymour and Wichita Falls, a distance of five or six miles, and he now runs his own ranch with his wife Sylvia, twenty-four thousand leased acres north of Alpine, where they and a business partner raise Mexican Corriente cattle, a breed popular for rodeo stock—"recreation cattle," Nelson calls them. As a young man he worked cattle for the Gage Holland Ranch at Marathon and the Stradley Gage Ranch south of Alpine, and he wrangled horses for Buck Newsome, who had the riding concession at Big Bend National Park in the 1960s. He ran the Willow Springs division of the Kokernot 06 Ranch for fifteen years, looking out for a herd of six hundred to one thousand cattle, fixing fences and corrals and tending wells. He eventually became a nationally known horse breaker, traveling every year to the King Ranch in South Texas and the Parker Ranch in Hawaii to start their young horses. There is not much about cowboy work Nelson does not know, although he says, "I don't call myself a cowboy—I don't think that's a title you can bestow on yourself—but maybe I'll do until one comes along."

When Nelson was growing up in the 1950s and 60s, the Victorian tradition of reciting poetry aloud was still alive in Seymour. "My mother read poetry aloud to me," he told me, "and I fell in love with Eugene Field and with something called 'Nothing Gold Can Stay' by Robert Frost." Later, in high school, students had to memorize and recite twenty lines of poetry. "My teacher was Miss Anita Wells, a Seymour girl, and I was in love with her and wanted to impress her, so instead of just twenty lines I told her that I had memorized all of Poe's 'The Raven' and wanted to recite that. She said that I could, but I would have to recite half of it on one day and half of it the next. She married a coach, which broke my heart." In addition to Poe, Nelson discovered Kipling, Robert Service, and Stephen Vincent Benet, all of whose poems are still part of his recitation repertoire, in high school.

Nelson did not start writing poetry until he was in the army, in a 101st Airborne reconnaissance platoon in Vietnam. "I wrote letters in the form of poems," he told me. "I don't have any of them now, I sent them all off." In 1985, while he was working on the 06, he read in the *Western Horseman* magazine about the first National Cowboy Poetry Gathering in Elko, Nevada. He didn't attend, but he later heard some of the poetry from it and thought, "You know what, I can do this and I can do some of it even better." He started writing, and Texas State Folklorist Pat Jasper sent some of his poems to the Elko organizers. He was invited to the 1986 gathering, and has been back nearly every year since then. He has now been writing poetry consistently for twenty-five years.

"All a person has to do to write is to read," he told me. "The more I write the more I want to read and the more I read the more I want to write." Nelson said that he carried three books with him all through his time in Vietnam, wrapped in plastic. They were A. B. Guthrie's novel *The Big Sky*, Aldo Leopold's *Sand County Almanac*, and Eric Hoffer's *The Passionate State of Mind*. He still has those three volumes on his bookshelf.

"I started out writing poems mostly about cowboy work," Nelson said, "but then I saw other poets like Wally McCrae and Paul Zarzyski writing not so much about what they were doing but what they were feeling, and I started writing outside of the box. Most of my writing now is free verse."

Poetry recitation, like cowboy work, requires a good deal of old-fashioned skill and lots of practice. Nelson still recites the classics as well as his own work at cowboy poetry gatherings all over the country as well as at the Texas Cowboy Poetry Gathering in Alpine, with which he has been involved since its founding. "I must have recited Stephen Vincent Benet's 'The Ballad of William Sycamore' a thousand times," he said. One of his favorites is his friend Buck Ramsey's "Anthem," a paean to the open range written in 1989. "When I memorized 'Anthem' I had to recite it dozens of times by myself before I could get through it without choking up," he told me. For Nelson, recitation is not just a matter of memorization. "I get inside the poem," he says. "I recite it from inside out, and then it's not a matter of remembering the words. They are just there."

Nelson is only the third cowboy poet to receive a National Heritage Fellowship (the other two were Wally McRae and Buck Ramsey) and the twelfth Texan (five of the other Texans were accordionists). In September he will go to Washington for a presentation ceremony on Capitol Hill and a banquet at the Library of Congress.

May 21, 2009

✣ 62 ✣

RANCH VERSES

William Lawrence Chittenden, *Ranch Verses*.
New York: G. P. Putnam's Sons, 1893.

THERE ARE two poems that every Texan of my parents' generation knew by heart and would recite at the drop of a hat. They are Frank Desprez's "Lasca" and Larry Chittenden's "The Cowboys' Christmas Ball." Not long ago I ran into Chuck Finsley, retired curator of paleontology at the Dallas Museum of Science, who was having lunch with my friend Evelyn Luciani at the Food Shark in Marfa. Finsley was in town to plan a bus tour of the Big Bend for a group of Dallasites, and he was trying to persuade Luciani to join the tour and recite "Lasca" as the bus rolled down US 67 from Marfa to Presidio. The poem, in the best sentimental Victorian tradition, is about a Texas rancher who is saved from a stampede by his lover, who throws her body over his and is trampled to death by the cattle. The last line goes, "Does half my heart lie buried there, down by the Rio Grande?"

But because Christmas is coming this column is about the other poem, "The Cowboys' Christmas Ball," which has detached itself from the printed page and taken on a life of its own. The poem, which describes a dance held in Anson City, Texas, in the late 1880s, was written by Larry Chittenden, a local rancher, and was first published in the Anson City newspaper, the *Texas Western*, in June 1890. The Star Hotel, where the dance was held, had just burned down, and the newspaper was seeking information about the hotel's history. "The Cowboys' Christmas Ball" was Chittenden's contribution. Three years later it was included in a volume of Chittenden's poetry called *Ranch Verses*, published by G. P. Putnam's Sons in New York. *Ranch Verses* went through sixteen printings and earned Chittenden the sobriquet "The Ranchman-Poet." It also brought "The Cowboys' Christmas Ball" to a national audience.

The poem, in six verses of jogging, slangy lines that are reminiscent of Robert Service's poems of the Far North, lends itself both to recitation and to singing. Someone probably set it to music soon after it was published because it appeared in the first book of cowboy songs, Jack Tharp's *Songs of the Cowboys* (1908). Tharp's book also included a knock-off of Chittenden's poem called "The Cowboys' New Year's Dance," set in Roswell, New Mexico, and supposedly written by Mark Chisholm, a clever pseudonym that calls up both Mark Twain and the Chisholm Trail. John A. Lomax included Chittenden's verses in the 1916 edition of his *Cowboy Songs*, saying that it "had been set to music by cowboys." In 1946 a cowboy singer named Gordon Graham wrote a new tune for it, and in 1985 Michael Martin Murphey made a hit recording of the song to that tune. The poem has also been reprinted hundreds of times in magazines, usually at Christmas, and it became a standard recitation piece at Christmas celebrations.

The Christmas dance that Chittenden described was held sporadically in Anson until prohibition. In 1934, however, a local English teacher, Leonora Barrett, aware of the poem's popularity, decided to revive the dance as a historical pageant. Barrett was a student of J. Frank Dobie's, and she had written her University of Texas master's thesis on "The Texas Cowboy in Literature." She organized a group of dancers who could perform waltzes, schottisches, reels, and polkas, dressed them in Victorian costumes, took over the high school gymnasium, and the Cowboys' Christmas Ball was reborn. Three years later Barrett took the dancers to the National Folk Festival in Chicago; they were such a hit that when the festival was held in Washington, DC, in 1938 they were invited to dance on the White House lawn. In 1940 the Works Progress Administration built a rock building, Pioneer Hall, as a permanent home for the ball, which still takes place there on three nights every December. Shortly after Michael Martin Murphey recorded the song he more or less adopted the ball, and his annual appearance there has swelled the number of dancers considerably.

Larry Chittenden, the poem's author and spiritual father of the ball, was hardly your typical Texas rancher. His father was a prominent New York dry goods merchant, and Chittenden started his career as a clerk in his father's store. He first came to Texas to manage a ranch in Jones County that his uncle, a congressman from New York, had bought. He stayed in Texas about fifteen years and then moved to Bermuda. There he produced another volume of poetry, *Bermuda Verses*, which contains lines like, "Bright land of lovely lilies, roses, and cedar trees / Enchantment dwells about thee and in thy emerald seas." "The Cowboys' Christmas Ball" may be his best poem. He ended up in Christmas Cove, Maine, where he established a public library of autographed books. He died in 1934.

This year's Cowboys' Christmas Ball will be held on December 16, 17, and 18. Suanne Holtman, who has been involved with the ball for eighteen years ("and I'm a newcomer," she says), tells me that there are still plenty of tickets at $15 each. However, there are certain rules that dancers must observe in order to preserve the decorum of the 1880s. Ladies must wear skirts on the dance floor (and no split skirts), and men must not dance with their hats on (there is a hat check booth). No alcohol is permitted, although Holtman says, "What people drink in their cars between dances is their own business." The ball is opened by a grand march, and the dances include waltzes, schottisches, Virginia reels, polkas, and a Paul Jones.

So get yourself to Anson City, "old Jones's county seat / Where they raised polled Angus cattle and waving whiskered wheat" and spend an evening at "that lively gaited sworray—the Cowboys' Christmas Ball!"

December 16, 2010

✣ 63 ✣

THE BOOK WE ALL LEARNED TEXAS HISTORY FROM

HAVE YOU EVER wondered why every Texan over forty knows the details of the Texas Revolution by heart and can tell you at the drop of a hat about the cannon at Gonzales, the Goliad massacre, Travis and the line in the sand at the Alamo, the Mier prisoners and the drawing of the black beans and the white beans, and the other stories that if Texas were still an independent republic would make up our national epic? These are not tales that were passed from generation to generation, because most Texans' ancestors were not here in the 1830s, when these events occurred. These stories owe their wide circulation to a little comic book called *Texas History Movies*, which every seventh grader in Texas got a free copy of, courtesy of the Magnolia Petroleum Company, from 1927 until 1960. Literally millions of copies were distributed.

The book was small, only five by seven inches, and was 128 pages long. The cover of the earlier editions showed a movie screen, with curtains drawn back around it and an enthralled audience sitting in front of it watching the Battle of the Alamo. The title, "Texas History Movies," was at the top, and below the audience were the words, "For Young and Old—Interesting & Instructive." Later editions had a simpler red, white, and blue cover. Each page had eight cartoon panels on it, framing a printed caption in the center. A preface explained the technique: "The pictures themselves tell the story and not the printed captions, which serve in the fashion of cinema sub-titles." (Remember that this was in the days of silent movies.) The panels themselves, drawn by cartoonist Jack Patton, were clean and simple but were packed with movement and telling detail. The captions were written by *Dallas Morning News* theater critic John Rosenfield Jr. The remarkable thing about the little booklet is that it was published several years before the first American comic books came on the market.

Texas History Movies had its origins in a daily Texas history comic strip produced by Patton and Rosenfield that first appeared in the *Dallas Morning News* in October 1926. The four-panel strip ran until June 1927, when it was suspended at the request of history teachers all over the state until school reopened in the fall. When the final installment appeared in June 1928, Patton and Rosenfield had produced 1,600 panels that made a lasting impression on the way Texans perceive their past.

The strength of *Texas History Movies* was that it used slang, colloquialisms, and deliberate anachronisms to humanize people from the past. In one memorable panel depicting Mexican soldiers and Austin colonists fraternizing over a game of horseshoes, a soldier about to toss a horseshoe says, "Watch this ringer, Señor Bill," and the colonist replies, "You're full of prunes, Pedro." One of its weaknesses was that to its authors "Texas history" clearly meant the settlement of Texas by Anglo-Americans and the subsequent revolution against Mexico. Over half of its pages were devoted to the years between 1821 and 1848. Another even worse weakness was that it made use of the racial stereotypes of the 1920s to caricature both African Americans and Hispanics in the cruelest of ways. The drawings and the language, viewed at the beginning of the twenty-first century, are almost unbelievable. As a result, it provided an extremely distorted view of Texas history. As novelist Larry McMurtry has said, its images "stopped two generations of public school students dead in their tracks as far as history is concerned." My friend James Crisp, a Texas historian languishing in exile at

North Carolina State University, has written feelingly in his book *Sleuthing the Alamo* about his own efforts to liberate himself from the effects of *Texas History Movies* as he became a professional historian.

In 1960, due partially to growing objections from African American and Hispanic groups, Magnolia Petroleum stopped distributing the booklet to schools and turned the copyright over to the Texas State Historical Association. The association, with the help of a multi-racial advisory group, made a well-intentioned effort to clean up the pictures and the text and get the publication back into the schools. Like many such efforts, this one went askew. The net result was that nearly every panel depicting an African American was eliminated, and caricature was replaced by complete absence. Language was altered beyond necessity, so that the horseshoe-pitching colonist's brash "You're full of prunes, Pedro," became an innocuous "I'm all eyes, friend." In a panel depicting an eighteenth-century Spanish governor kicking a cat in fury at receiving bad news, the cat was removed with Wite-Out correcting fluid, leaving the governor with one foot inexplicably in the air. In 1984 the association proudly reported that 100,000 copies of the revised booklet had been distributed to schools and not one complaint had been received, but some of the essential vinegar had gone out of the publication. What was needed was not a sanitized version of the old booklet but a completely new start from different assumptions.

I am happy to say that has now happened. The Texas State Historical Association has just published *New Texas History Movies,* written and drawn by Texas historian-artist Jack Jackson. The handsome little book is only forty-eight pages long, but it covers Texas history from the arrival of the Spanish in the Americas to the 1880s, and it has none of the flaws of the old volume. Although the irreverent tone of the original book is retained in the text of the new one, Hispanics, Native Americans, and African Americans are presented as active participants in Texas history, and they are depicted with dignity and humanity. While the old book focused largely on the Texas Revolution, Jackson, who died last summer, devoted the first third of the book to the Spanish and Mexican periods, and the Revolution only gets six pages. This is understandable, as Jackson was not only an accomplished artist who started drawing underground comic books in the 1960s but a self-taught scholar whose books on Spanish and Mexican Texas are considered the definitive word on their subjects. *New Texas History Movies* is a fitting memorial to his genius, and it is fun to read, too.

March 22, 2007

✣ 64 ✣

THE ROTARIANS' BOOK FESTIVAL

I HAVE ALWAYS BEEN suspicious of Rotary Clubs and Rotarians, having been brought up by parents who shared all of H. L. Mencken's prejudices against civic boosters, and in the 1970s I had those prejudices confirmed by having to become a member of the Downtown Dallas Rotary Club as a condition of employment with the Dallas Historical Society. The Downtown Dallas Rotarians were cigar-smoking Republican businessmen who threw rolls at each other during lunch. But this bias was completely swept away Saturday before last, when I attended the first Way Out West Texas Book Festival, sponsored by the Alpine Rotary Club as part of Rotary International's campaign for literacy. The festival was organized by the Rotarians with the help of the Alpine Public Library and Front Street Books, and it was a bang-up success.

The best thing about the Way Out West Festival was its size. It was small enough to fit into the second floor of Sul Ross's Espino Conference Center, and, unlike Austin's mammoth Texas Book Festival, it provided plenty of opportunities to visit face-to-face with your favorite author. My favorite of the day was Denise Chavez, author of *Face of an Angel*, which won the American Book Award in 1995. Chavez was promoting her recent book, *A Taco Testimony*, a book of essays about family and food interspersed with poems, recipes, and photographs. Chavez, who is a woman of a certain age, radiated earthy energy. She gave her keynote address wearing a t-shirt that had "Make Tacos Not War" printed across it, black slacks, a chef's apron, and a beret. On a table in front of her were boxes and packages of lard, sugar, and spices, which she gave away as door prizes at the end of her talk.

Chavez has a BA in drama and was a student of Paul Baker's at the Dallas Theater Center in the 1970s, and her address was more like a vaudeville performance than a lecture. She told stories about her mother, recited poetry, and gave out a recipe for *capirotada sin verguenza* (shameless bread pudding) which involved last week's flour tortillas, raisins and pecans, piloncillo, pineapple juice, and "anything old and ugly in your refrigerator that will soften up and taste good again." She interviewed members of the audience about their experiences eating dog food, cajoled a cousin who was there into telling about his visit to his grandfather's grave in Redford, and led everyone in what she called the taco cheer ("T is for tacos, A is for awesome, C is *para la comida de mi gente . . .*").

While Chavez was born and grew up in Las Cruces, New Mexico, she has roots in the Big Bend. Her mother, Delfina Rede Faver de Chavez, was born in Redford, and was Enrique Madrid's aunt. Her mother's first husband, Tiburcio Faver, was a descendant of the legendary Big Bend rancher Milton Faver. Certainly there is enough material in *A Taco Testimony* about Redford and Ojinaga to qualify it as a Big Bend book.

Joe Nick Patoski, who is known to many in the Big Bend for his beautiful books with Laurence Parent, *Texas Mountains* and *Big Bend National Park*, was the runner-up for my favorite (as he got up from the table where we had been chatting after Chavez's performance he muttered, "Don't ever follow the elephant act"). In addition to writing about the Texas landscape, Patoski has written about Texas music, and he has just followed biographies of Selena and Stevie Ray Vaughn with a five-hundred-page biography of Willie Nelson. Actually, it is 497 pages; he told me that his publisher told him that reader interest lagged after five hundred pages. He later discovered that after five hundred pages the price of a book goes up $10.00, making it much harder to sell.

This is the kind of inside information you can pick up at a book festival.

Patoski needn't have worried about following the elephant act. He is a small, wiry fellow, and he literally vibrated with enthusiasm as he was interviewed by KRTS's Drew Stuart about his Willie Nelson book. He explained that he really started out to write a book about Texas because, he said, "I moved to Fort Worth at the age of two from Allentown, Pennsylvania, and I've been trying to figure Texas out ever since." Texans, he said, "have an experience with the sacred and profane that transcends anyplace else in the US—we get drunk in beer joints every Saturday night and show up at the Baptist church every Sunday morning and don't acknowledge the people we got drunk with the night before." When Patoski pitched the idea of a Texas book to his agent, the agent suggested that he tell the story through somebody, and Patoski realized that Willie Nelson was "the emblematic Texan."

"The key to understanding Willie," Patoski told his audience, "is that at heart he is a salesman. When he was trying to break into the music business he sold encyclopedias, carpeting, vacuum cleaners, and he knows that he has to sell himself before he can sell his product. He is the only musician I've ever interviewed that maintained eye contact with me all through the interview."

There were other speakers, too. Sarah Bird kept an audience convulsed while she talked about creating humorous characters and her encounters with Alpine traffic cops, and there were panels on a variety of topics. There was even a silent auction to benefit the Alpine Public Library, at which my wife managed to buy a nearly complete eight-place setting of Franciscan Desert Rose china, a pattern she has wanted to own since she was eight. But the best part of the festival was the opportunity to talk with other writers about the frustrations of writing and the compensatory pleasures of reading.

Tom Michael of KRTS, who is on the Alpine Library Board,

told me the best story of the day. It seems that an elderly gentleman walked into the Alpine Public Library one day and told the librarian that he had read only one book in his life, the Bible, and that he would like to read another before he died. There was a copy of James Michener's *Texas* lying on the librarian's desk, and so she suggested that. He took it to a table and started reading, and he came back every day until he finished. He handed it back to the librarian and said, "That was pretty good. Has that man written any other books?"

It just goes to show that you are never too old to start reading.

August 21, 2008

Photo by Bill Wright

LONN TAYLOR is a historian and writer who retired to Fort Davis, Texas, with his wife, Dedie, after twenty years as a historian at the Smithsonian Institution's National Museum of American History in Washington, DC. He received a BA in history and government from Texas Christian University in 1961 and did graduate work at New York University before returning to Texas to enter the museum field. He served as curator and director of the University of Texas at Austin's Winedale Historical Center from 1970 to 1977; as curator of history at the Dallas Historical Society from 1977 to 1979; and as curator and deputy director of the Museum of New Mexico in Santa Fe from 1980 to 1984. Taylor's books include *Texas Furniture: The Cabinetmakers and Their Work, 1840-1880* (with David Warren, University of Texas Press, 1975, revised edition, 2012); *The American Cowboy* (with Ingrid Maar, Library of Congress, 1983); *New Mexican Furniture, 1600-1940* (with Dessa Bokides, Museum of New Mexico Press, 1987); *The Star-Spangled Banner: The Flag That Inspired the National Anthem* (Harry N. Abrams, 2000); *The Star-Spangled Banner: The Making of an American Icon* (with Kathleen Kendrick and Jeffrey Brodie, Smithsonian Books, 2008); *Texas, My Texas: Musings of the Rambling Boy* (TCU Press, 2012); and *Texas People, Texas Places: More Musings of the Rambling Boy* (TCU Press, 2014). He writes a weekly column about Texas called The Rambling Boy, for the Marfa *Big Bend Sentinel.*